ADVANCE PRAISE FOR
Soul Training with the Peace Prayer of Saint Francis

We live in a world of high anxiety where talk of peace is obscured by a noisy culture of chaos. Francis of Assisi also lived in tumultuous times but turned his life around, from the darkness of worldly greed toward the light of God's generous love. In the wellspring of God's love, he found the deep joy of peace. Father Albert Haase has given us a workbook of conversion, following Francis's spiritual path. Drawing from personal stories and Franciscan spirituality, Father Haase illumines the Peace Prayer as a way of turning from darkness to light, from anxiety and distress to the deep peace of God's love. Each chapter concludes with a thoughtful "training workout" and reflection points to consider, as the soul is shaped in love. In an age of body workouts and exercise regimens, training the soul for peace may be one of the most important routines we take up on a committed basis. For there can be no peace in the world unless there is peace in the heart.

—Sr. Ilia Delio, OSF,
Josephine Connelly Endowed Chair in Theology,
Villanova University

Inspired! Father Albert Haase takes us on a panoramic tour into the human drama using the verses of the Prayer attributed to St Francis. With each phrase of the prayer, Father Haase opens up a dimension of human pain and invites us to see the lives of those who have not only suffered but found spiritual freedom. Most interesting to me as a third order Franciscan are the stories from Francis's life that illustrate how this great saint emptied himself of all privilege and power in order to be transformed by the suffering. In this volume the reader encounters real people's stories, including the author's, the examples of numerous saints, and the spiritual principles that lead to a life of joy in following Jesus.

—FR DAVE SCHEIDER,
Episcopal priest, spiritual director, member of
The Third Order Society of St. Francis (Episcopal)

Using the Franciscan Peace Prayer as a framework and foundation, Fr. Albert through his own specifically designed method of storytelling and reflection, has written a book that is an invaluable resource for anyone who is serious about their spiritual life. The spiritual journey calls for discipline and commitment and this amazing book offers a guide for those who are searching to live a more authentic life in the Spirit.

—DR. C. VANESSA WHITE
Associate Professor of Spirituality and Ministry
Catholic Theological Union

The BE Attitudes: Ten Paths to Holiness (DVD) (Paraclete Press, 2019)

Practical Holiness: Pope Francis as Spiritual Companion (Paraclete Press, 2019)

Becoming an Ordinary Mystic: Spirituality for the Rest of Us (InterVarsity Press, 2019)

Soul Training
with the
Peace Prayer
of Saint Francis

• • •

ALBERT HAASE, O.F.M.

franciscan
media®
Cincinnati, Ohio

Scripture passages have been taken from New Revised Standard Version Bible, copyright ©1989 by the Division of Christian Education of the National Council of the Churches of Christ in the U.S.A., and used by permission. All rights reserved. Excerpts from *St. Francis of Assisi: Writings and Early Biographies. English Omnibus of the Sources for the Life of St. Francis*, ed. Marion A. Habig, Copyright © 1972 used with permission of Franciscan Media.Some material originally appeared in *Instruments of Christ: Reflections on the Peace Prayer of St. Francis of Assisi* (St. Anthony Messenger Press, 2004)

LIBRARY OF CONGRESS CATALOGING-IN-PUBLICATION DATA
Names: Haase, Albert, 1955- author.
Title: Soul training with the peace prayer of Saint Francis / Albert Haase, O.F.M.
Description: Cincinnati, Ohio : Franciscan Media, 2020. | Summary: "Using stories of ordinary people working to grow in their spirituality, Franciscan Father Albert Haase illuminates each phrase of the Peace Prayer commonly attributed to Saint Francis of Assisi"-- Provided by publisher.
Identifiers: LCCN 2020030127 (print) | LCCN 2020030128 (ebook) | ISBN 9781632533494 (acid-free paper) | ISBN 9781632533500 (epub)
Subjects: LCSH: Prayer of St. Francis of Assisi.
Classification: LCC BV284.P73 H336 2020 (print) | LCC BV284.P73 (ebook) | DDC 242/.7--dc23
LC record available at https://lccn.loc.gov/2020030127
LC ebook record available at https://lccn.loc.gov/2020030128

Cover and book design by Mark Sullivan

Published by Franciscan Media
28 W. Liberty St.
Cincinnati, OH 45202
www.FranciscanMedia.org

Printed in the United States of America.
Printed on acid-free paper.
20 21 22 23 24   5 4 3 2 1

....

"Do you not know that in a race the runners all compete,
but only one receives the prize?
Run in such a way that you may win it.
Athletes exercise self-control in all things;
they do it to receive a perishable wreath,
but we an imperishable one."
— 1 CORINTHIANS 9:24–25

....

CONTENTS

....

When he was a high school seminarian, Father Albert ended one of our spiritual direction sessions with, "Father Murray, you are soon going on a long journey that will be the fulfillment of the dream of your life." I already knew I was soon to travel to Assisi to write a life of St. Francis. Albert could not have known that, nor could he have known the part his prescient words would play in the theme of the book that became *Francis: The Journey and the Dream.* His words confirmed the direction the book was already taking. And now, reading his book on praying and living the Peace Prayer of St. Francis, I realize his words are again prescient. They could change the direction of anyone's life who takes to heart the words of this Peace Prayer and begins to live them. The words of the prayer can train the soul to be as fit as so many people's bodies are in today's gym-oriented world. This book is a challenge and an exciting spiritual journey for anyone who longs for true peace of soul and for peace in our world.

I am writing these words at a time of great suffering and confusion in America. The coronavirus is raging, a silent chaotic disease that is inside the increasingly loud outer protests against that other disease that is consuming America: racism. These two diseases mirror each other in that they are both bred in silence and erupt into the body politic when the silence that preceded them becomes a subtle and sometimes not so subtle denial that something is deeply wrong inside America. It is becoming more and more evident that justice and transparency have been denied those who are begging for justice and those who are demanding the truth about COVID-19, the viral disease that is killing so many Americans. In a sense these two diseases are both viral, and they cannot be defined and defeated unless we begin to love one another as God loves us, without prejudice or favoritism, but, as St. Francis says, "as a mother loves and nourishes her own child." Using the Peace Prayer of St. Francis, Fr. Albert once again predicts that if we embrace this prayer, we will all begin to embark on a long journey that will result in the fulfillment of our deepest dream.

Fr. Albert was but a mere boy when he predicted the journey I was beginning into the dream of Assisi and its most famous son, Francis Bernardone, who became the symbol of what it means to be at peace with God and others. Now Fr. Albert is but a humble Franciscan friar speaking out about a way all of us can be led by the spirituality of St. Francis and find the peace which even democracy seems to keep denying large portions of American society, especially among the poor, the disenfranchised, the people who because of their color have continued to be oppressed and dismissed since the beginning of slavery in America and even before that since the beginning of America's riding roughshod over the lands and rights and dignity of its own indigenous peoples.

Nancy Pelosi, the Speaker of the United States House of Representatives, said something in an interview on television that to me pinpointed what a book like this does for the reader who takes it to heart. She said that people often ask her, "Where is hope?" And she answers them that hope is where it always was, between faith and charity. Faith leads to hope in the goodness of others, which is shown in charity, or love for one another. Faith, hope, and charity are the only way to peace. I can't think of a better manual than the Peace Prayer of Saint Francis to guide us to become peaceful people, both personally and as a society.

Lord, make us instruments of your peace.

—Murray Bodo, OFM
July 2020

" ...I thank you for the words of Saint Francis of Assisi, whose prayer my husband and I carry with us both in our home in East Nashville and in our work across rural Africa...As we enter this election season, I pray Saint Francis's words for us all. Lord, make us instruments of your peace..."[1]

Author and HIV/AIDS activist Jena Lee Nardella so ended the closing Benediction on the opening night of the 2012 Democratic National Convention.

Why does the Peace Prayer of Saint Francis cast such a magical spell on people? The list of people who have referred to and even prayed it reads like a *Who's Who* of potential saints and power brokers. Famous religious people have prayed it and encouraged others to do the same: Francis Joseph Cardinal Spellman handed out copies at his installation as archbishop of New York on May 23, 1939 and asked that the prayer be sung at Pope Paul VI's Mass in Yankee Stadium on October 4, 1965; the official medal he commissioned for that papal visit of peace to the United Nations has the first verse of the prayer engraved on one side. Mother Teresa of Calcutta included it in the morning prayers for the religious community she founded, the Missionaries of Charity; she passed out copies and had those in attendance pray it together when she received the Nobel Peace Prize on December 10, 1979, in Oslo, Norway. South African Archbishop Desmond Tutu, the 1984 Nobel Peace Prize laureate, made it part of his religious devotions. Hosting religious leaders from around the world, Pope John Paul II prayed the Peace Prayer at the conclusion of the 1986 World Day of Prayer for Peace in Assisi, Italy.

Politicians also have invoked it: Margaret Thatcher, after winning the 1979 United Kingdom general election, referred to four paraphrased lines of the Peace Prayer as "particularly apt at the moment"[2] in her first news conference as prime minister. Congressman Peter Rodino of New Jersey, who served as chairman of the House Judiciary Committee during the impeachment inquiry of President Richard Nixon, prayed the Peace Prayer every day of his life.[3] Welcoming Pope John Paul II for his fourth visit to the United States on October 4, 1995, President Bill Clinton mentioned how the Peace Prayer is carried "in the pockets, the purses, the billfolds of many American Catholics and revered by many who are not Catholic"[4] and then quoted the first two verses. Nancy Pelosi, becoming the first woman to be elected Speaker of the U.S. House of Representatives on January 2, 2007, thanked her constituents in San Francisco and California by referring to "our city's anthem" and explicitly paraphrasing the prayer, "Lord, make me a channel of thy peace; where there is darkness may we bring light, where there is hatred, may we bring love, and where there is despair, may we bring hope,"[5] and again quoted the first line of "our anthem"[6] on January 3, 2019, when she regained the gavel. At the September 25, 2015 press conference announcing his resignation from Congress after twenty-five years of service, Ohio Republican John Boehner read it.[7]

People turn to this prayer on solemn occasions, be they somber or joyful: the Royal British Legion's annual Festival of Remembrance that commemorates all those who died in conflicts; the funerals of Diana, Princess of Wales, and Mother Teresa of Calcutta; the marriage of Prince Albert II of Monaco.

South African songwriter Sebastian Temple's 1967 musical rendition, "Make Me a Channel of Your Peace," continues to enjoy immense popularity among the more than fifteen renditions by various musicians. Versions of the prayer are sung or recited in Franco Zeffirelli's 1972 film about Saint Francis, *Brother Sun, Sister Moon*, an early trailer for Sylvester Stallone's 2008 film *Rambo*, the eleventh episode of season 1 of HBO's *Deadwood*, the 2013 Canadian musical *Come from Away*, and the 2017 movie *Lady Bird*. Some scholars raised an eyebrow when the executive producers of *The Sultan and the Saint*, a documentary about the encounter between Sultan Malik al-Kamil of Egypt and Saint Francis of Assisi that premiered on PBS in December 2017, couldn't resist including a scene of the saint praying the prayer that probably was composed seven hundred years after his death! (See Appendix 1 for the history of how the Peace Prayer became associated with Saint Francis.)

In his message to journalists for World Communications Day on January 24, 2018, Pope Francis addressed the issue of "fake news" and challenged all journalists to promote a "journalism of peace."[8] He concluded his message with a revision of the Peace Prayer that was slanted toward journalism. (See Appendix 4 for this version for journalists.)

Artists have written the Peace Prayer in intricate calligraphy. Monks and nuns have mounted it on plaques and sold it in gift shops. Grandmothers have cross-stitched it and given it as gifts.

Why has this prayer enjoyed an unparalleled popularity in the past one hundred years? Why do princess and pauper, bishop and bellhop, saint and sinner turn to it in emotionally charged moments of life?

SOUL TRAINING AND THE PHYSICS OF THE PEACE PRAYER

A number of years ago, while preaching a retreat to some Franciscan friars in Pennsylvania, I got a possible answer to those questions from a surprising source: a young friar, thirty years my junior.

Brother Angelo had been in the Franciscan Order for five years and, by his own admission, was "a big fan of the Peace Prayer." He was well aware that Saint Francis did not compose the prayer "and that doesn't bother me in the least. I still pray it slowly every single day and let the words wash over me. By trying to put this prayer into action, I feel like I am training my soul to be both a healthy disciple of Jesus and a faithful follower of Francis."

Holding a master's degree in physics, Brother Angelo enthusiastically added, "I just love the physics of the Peace Prayer!"

"The *physics* of the Peace Prayer? What do you mean?"

This prayer challenges the spiritual laws of our human nature. Because of sin, my natural inclination is to focus always on myself. I tend to be self-absorbed and self-centered. I fuss about *me*, *my* desires, *my* wants, and *my* demands. I can't break free from the ego's strong gravitational pull.

I liken it to what is called in physics the centripetal force. If you put a stone on a string and whirl it around your head, the string is constantly trying to pull the stone toward the center. *I'm* the center, and life is all about me.

The second part of the Peace Prayer is a reminder that it's not about me being the center and not about being consoled, understood, or loved. It's not about me receiving or being forgiven. The prayer shapes the contours of the soul to forget the ego and be selfless—that's how you cross the finish line to eternal life.

Physics also deals with what's called the centrifugal force. The stone on a string that you are whirling around your head is always trying to break free and move beyond the center. It's as if it wants to break free from the gravitational pull of the self and move outward and beyond.

That's really what the first part of the Peace Prayer is all about. It trains the soul to look outward and beyond, to be sensitive to every situation, and to bring whatever is needed to help those who are injured, doubtful, depressed, or struggling to find light or joy. Service—the point of the first stanza of the prayer—leads to selflessness—the point of the second stanza of the prayer—and vice versa. That's how the two parts of the Peace Prayer are related.

That's why I am a big fan of the Peace Prayer even if Saint Francis didn't compose it. It not only gets me in spiritual shape by focusing my attention on others but also keeps me in shape by challenging me to die to my natural inclinations.

Athletes talk about being in the zone; when I'm doing selfless acts of service and not thinking about myself, I'm in that sacred zone where God fashions his instruments.

Cleverly combining physics with athletics, Brother Angelo's explanation revealed the perennial attraction and appeal of the Peace Prayer.

Soul Training with the Peace Prayer of Saint Francis will show you how this simple prayer can train the soul and keep you in shape until you cross the finish line into eternal life. Think of this book as your workout manual that offers encouragement to condition all the muscles of the virtues to help you stay spiritually fit: faith, hope, love, forgiveness, joy, consolation, understanding, and selflessness.

Questions at the end of each chapter tailor your workout routine and are offered for your personal reflection or for sharing with your book club or study group. A Scripture passage, a Franciscan passage, and a short prayer, all offered as a spiritual "cooldown" after your workout, conclude each chapter.

You'll meet some spiritual athletes in these pages who are my spiritual directees, family members, or friends. I've changed their names and details of their stories to ensure their privacy.

After reading *Soul Training with the Peace Prayer of Saint Francis*, you'll know why pontiffs, presidents, politicians, paralegals, plumbers, and proofreaders keep turning to the Peace Prayer: it gets you in the zone where God's grace shapes and stretches your soul, transforming you into a saint who shimmers and shines.

—Albert Haase, OFM

Feast of Saint Francis of Assisi

THE PEACE PRAYER OF SAINT FRANCIS OF ASSISI

Lord, make me an instrument of your peace.
Where there is hatred, let me sow love;
where there is injury, pardon;
where there is doubt, faith;
where there is despair, hope;
where there is darkness, light;
and where there is sadness, joy.

O Divine Master, grant that I may not so much seek
to be consoled as to console;
to be understood as to understand;
to be loved as to love.
For it is in giving that we receive;
it is in pardoning that we are pardoned;
and it is in dying that we are born to eternal life.
Amen.

CHAPTER ONE

Lord and Divine Master

"I was sitting on the back porch with my morning cup of coffee. As I watched the dog sniff around the garden, a thought shot across my consciousness. *You've made enough money to last a lifetime and a half. Why don't you quit your job and consider using your computer skills and expertise to help inner city students? That could be a meaningful way to spend the next part of your life.* I had no idea where this thought came from, and it caught me off guard. I've always been intent on working hard and making money so I could enjoy a comfortable retirement. And the fact is: I really enjoy my job and am proud of my professional success. I've also made some wise financial investments. So I didn't pay any attention to that thought. I just treated it like a distraction, like one of those thoughts that zips around your mind and then disappears."

I impulsively responded to my spiritual directee: "That probably was a wise decision. You can't trust and follow every single thought or idea that comes out of nowhere and pops into your consciousness."

"Well, that's not the end of the story," Blake continued, a flush creeping across his cheeks. "That idea started turning up again and again whenever I would relax or didn't have to concentrate on something. I would be cooking a meal. I would be watching television. I would be taking a shower. And suddenly it would return. *Quit the job. Use your computer skills to help inner city kids.* The thought kept nagging me. The more I swatted it away, the more it would return. The more it returned, the more I realized again I have enough money for the future. I gradually lost interest in my professional success. *Is God asking something of me? Jesus, is this really what you want me to do?* After all, Father, as you know from the past few years, my greatest desire is to do God's will and by his grace, become a saint."

Our spiritual direction session came to an end on that note. Though I didn't tell Blake, I suspected this thought was one of those passing fancies that we all experience from time to time when we think we should be doing something more for God or want to deepen our spiritual growth. Those fancies are often self-generated and not Spirit-guided.

Six weeks later, Blake was sitting across from me again. He likes to begin his spiritual direction sessions with prayer, so I invited him to get us started. His prayer was surprisingly short. "Thank you, Lord. Let it be done to me according to your will."

Having been Blake's spiritual director for four years, I knew something was up. I smiled and asked, "What was *that* all about?"

"I did it. I resigned from the firm. I still can't believe it," he said as he shook his head. "I could have kept working there for the next fifteen years when I would be eligible for early retirement, but for what? What would be the point? I have more than enough to live on, thanks to my investments. It's time for me to look beyond myself. For some strange, inexplicable reason, my gut tells me that God is calling me to help disadvantaged kids with my computer skills. So if that is what God is asking of me, it's time to give it a shot. I contacted Catholic Charities and they put me in touch with Go Up Higher, an organization that helps high school students from low-income families aim for college. I've only been there for two weeks. I must say, Father, it's a bit of a challenge. It's stretching me in ways I've never been stretched before. But I think this is what God wants me to do. Odd, huh? I'm so grateful to you for helping me respond to God's call."

Now *I* felt a flush creeping across *my* cheeks. I hadn't done anything; if anything, I might have discouraged Blake from making the change. I stood in admiration of his valiant, selfless sacrifice in answer to what he thought was God's invitation and call. Much to my embarrassment and shame, I quickly realized that I needed to follow Blake's lead and make God the Lord and Divine Master of my life.

A Crisis and Transition

It's natural for all of us to spend the first thirty to forty years of life getting ourselves established both personally and professionally. By age forty, many of us have already decided on the single or married life and whether to become a parent. Many of us also spend these years climbing the ladder of success in hopes of attaining financial security and recognition in our careers. The centripetal force that Brother Angelo spoke about in this book's introduction is operative: we're focused on ourselves, our wishes and wants, and perhaps on the dream of making a mark and leaving a legacy.

These years also are governed by the personality props we think we need in order to be happy. Personality props are those external things that we lean on and that help define our self-worth and self-image: things like power, prestige, possessions, popularity, pleasure, and praise. Though there is nothing inherently wrong with such props—they enhance our emotional health and well-being—some people lean heavily on them and believe they cannot survive without them.

The reason why people lean heavily on the personality props and sometimes become obsessed with them is often rooted in a childhood trauma or deficiency: what they lacked or *think* they lacked in childhood becomes transformed into the adult personality prop. Follow a twenty-something or thirty-something on Facebook or Twitter, and you'll quickly see how people enjoy posting—and bragging—about their props. Those posts often betray an actual or perceived unmet childhood need.

Somewhere in our late twenties, thirties, or early forties, however, something begins to shift inside us. A dissatisfaction with life or a gnawing restlessness rears its head. We begin to suspect that the ladder we've been climbing might be against the wrong wall. The personality props that once captivated our attention lose their attraction and sparkle. This typically is referred to as the midlife crisis or the midlife transition; each term highlights an important aspect of this experience.

As a crisis, everything is up for grabs as we grapple with the proverbial question, "Is this all there is to life?" We second-guess the decisions we so clearly and easily made years before. We become discontent with the lifestyle that once provided happiness. We become bored with the people who once held our interest and maybe even our hearts. We wonder where our life is going.

Sadly, some people in midlife remain stuck in this crisis mode. They turn in on themselves and make rash decisions that only exacerbate the emotional struggle they are experiencing. Margaret walked away from twenty-two years of marriage to pursue a relationship with a coworker that lasted only two years. Philip was devastated when the excitement of buying a motorcycle for himself quickly wore off, and he found himself restless again.

Some people are held captive by the centripetal force of the ego and the attachment and lure of the personality props.

As a transition, midlife can gradually shift the operative force in our lives from the centripetal to the centrifugal: we stretch and look beyond ourselves—to God and others. We start volunteering at a food pantry, church, or after-school tutorial program. For some of us, this is the time when we first become personally invested in the spiritual life. Though he had had an earlier interest in the spiritual life, it was only in his mid-forties that Blake started a serious regimen of training his soul for the long haul.

FRANCIS OF ASSISI

Of course, this doesn't always happen in our third or fourth decade. It can happen earlier thanks to the gratuity of God's grace. One of the biographies of Saint Francis suggests just this. According to an early biographer, Francis was only twenty years old when the chivalric spirit captivated and consumed him. He yearned to become a famous, accomplished knight. Signing up for Assisi's battle with the neighboring town of Perugia, he fought in combat near what is now known as the town of Collestrada. Francis was taken prisoner and would be confined to a dungeon for about a year before his father ransomed him.

We do not know how Francis passed that year in prison. But upon his release, he was sickly and depressed. His mother would help nurse him back to health.

Francis couldn't let go of the dream of being a prestigious knight. That was the personality prop he had leaned on for all his life. So he followed Walter of Brienne to southern Italy. It was in the town of Spoleto where the future saint had a dream that would pose both a crisis and transition for him.

"Francis," God asked, "whom is it better to follow? The Master or the servant?"

"The Master, of course," he replied.

"Why then," God asked, "do you worry to follow the servant and not the Master?"

"What do you want me to do, Lord?"

"Return to Assisi. This life is not intended for you."

And with that, Francis's military ambition went up in smoke as the operative force in his life began to shift from the centripetal to the centrifugal, and his fundamental stance changed from selfishness to selflessness. His soul training had begun. Later in his life, he would refer to this change as following "in the footsteps of your Son."[9]

MASTER OR SERVANT?

The first words of the two stanzas of the Peace Prayer—"Lord...O Divine Master..."—challenge the centripetal selfishness that is operative in my early life. They stretch me beyond the limits of my skin where the personality props of power, prestige, possessions, popularity, pleasure, and praise command my attention, admiration, and affection. They shame me with the realization that the world doesn't revolve around me, and happiness is not about my commands, desires, and wishes being satisfied. They imply the very question that Francis was asked in the dream, "Whom is it better to follow? The Master or the servant?" It was the very question that confronted Blake.

To serve the Lord and Divine Master is to recognize the gratuity of grace that is never exhausted and never expires: everything in my life is a grace, gift, and blessing. In the presence of God, I can claim absolutely nothing as my own—except my sin. My life is at the disposal of Jesus. Detached from my pride and indifferent to the personality props, I am constantly asked to serve him by responding to the unmet need or required duty of the present moment: that might be a prayer of praise or petition, a response to someone in need, an act of forgiveness, or the offer of an apology. As happened to Blake, the operating force in my life begins to shift to the centrifugal: Jesus is the Master, and I look beyond myself to serve him and follow in his footsteps.

During the final months of his life as he looked back over twenty years of serving the Lord and Divine Master, Francis of Assisi was keenly aware that the Lord was the divine almsgiver who had provided for him time and again. His life had been awash in God's grace. No less than six times in his Testament, he referred to the action of God's grace that had shaped his unique vision of gospel living: It was the Lord who inspired him to change the point of reference in his life from himself to others. It was the Lord who led him to live and serve the lepers. It was the Lord who gave him faith to pray in churches and to respect even the most sinful of priests. And it was the Lord who sent him brothers and revealed to him how to live the Gospel. The Master always provides the grace and strength to respond to divine requests. Soul training begins and ends with the gratuity of grace.

Abraham and Mary

The Bible presents numerous people who trained their souls and responded to the grace of serving the Lord and Divine Master. One Old Testament man and one New Testament woman stand out. Choosing the Master over the servant with a stunning obedience and generous sacrifice, each presents a challenge and encouragement for those of us who are serious about soul training.

The twenty-second chapter of Genesis begins with a heartbreaking, shocking, and excruciating story. God asks Abraham not to murder his beloved son, Isaac, but to sacrifice him—to return God's gift. Abraham's unflinching obedience is again highlighted; the story parallels the patriarch's earlier, first act of obedience when God called him away from his own country and father's house. In both situations, Abraham is told to go some-where (12:1; 22:2); in both situations, his faithful, unquestioning response elicits a promise from God (12:7; 22:17).

This is not the first time Abraham is asked to put one of his children in harm's way. In the previous chapter of Genesis, Sarah is insulted and threatened by Hagar and her son, Ishmael, whom the slave woman bore for Abraham. Her demand to send Hagar and Ismael away distresses Abraham. But God instructs Abraham to comply with Sarah's request, and so the patriarch obeys, sending Hagar and Ishmael off into the desert. The parallels to the story with Isaac are evident: both sons are placed in dangerous conditions (21:10; 22:2); Abraham's obedience is noted (21:14; 22:3); both sons will give birth to a nation (21:12–13; 22:17); an angel intervenes to alleviate any danger (21:17; 22:11–12).

One can't help but realize that with each increasingly difficult request—the call to leave Haran at seventy-five years of age, the sending away of his child fathered with a slave woman, and the sacrifice of his beloved son—Abraham gradually was training his soul with heroic obedience and steadfast trust even as God's grace was shaping the contours of his soul in selflessness. He had found the Lord and Divine Master to serve.

Luke's Gospel presents Mary as another biblical figure who chose to serve the Master. In first-century Judaism, a woman was considered a second-class citizen. She could own no property. As a matter of fact, she was considered property herself: she was owned by her parents, and, once married, she became the property of her husband. The only thing a woman could consider her own was her reputation.

The angel Gabriel entered this virgin's life and asked her to give up this one thing she could call her own: "Do not be afraid, Mary, for you have found favor with God. And now, you will conceive in your womb and bear a son, and you will name him Jesus" (Luke 1:30–31). Mary did not hesitate to respond. Her generosity erupted from within as she chose the Master over the servant, "Here am I, the servant of the Lord; let it be with me according to your word" (1:38). Word of her tarnished reputation must have quickly circulated, because we are told in the following verse that she set out "and went with haste to a Judean town in the hill country" (1:39).

Mary must have been too young to develop a taste for the personality prop of her reputation. Indeed, she renounced its centripetal pull and, by her own free decision, placed her life at the service of the Lord in selfless surrender and sacrifice.

Divided Hearts

Abraham and Mary teach us two important lessons about soul training: Abraham's story reminds us that we train our souls in steps and stages; small steps lead to larger strides. To serve God in obedience is not a one-time decision but is chosen time and again. Mary's story reminds us that serving the Master comes with a personal price: generosity and selflessness call us to renounce greed and selfishness.

I would be naïve to suggest that serving the Lord and Divine Master simply happens by the snap of a finger and a mere act of the will. Biblical stories sometimes mistakenly lead us to think just that. Only the inexperienced and immature would believe training the soul in the service of the Lord and Divine Master is an easy decision. The reality is far more complicated—and convoluted.

One of the great challenges in the spiritual life is learning to maneuver around our duplicitous desires. We often find ourselves standing between the Master and the servant and sometimes leaning toward one, at other times toward the other. Juxtaposing the centripetal pull of the servant (what the apostle calls "flesh,"

"the law of sin," and "members") and the centrifugal pull of the
Master ("inmost self," "mind," and "law of God"), Paul captured
the harsh reality of soul training and its internal struggle when he
wrote:

> I do not understand my own actions. For I do not do what I
> want, but I do the very thing I hate. Now if I do what I do not
> want, I agree that the law is good. But in fact it is no longer
> I that do it, but sin that dwells within me. For I know that
> nothing good dwells within me, that is, in my flesh. I can will
> what is right, but I cannot do it. For I do not do the good I
> want, but the evil I do not want is what I do. Now if I do what
> I do not want, it is no longer I that do it, but sin that dwells
> within me. So I find it to be a law that when I want to do what
> is good, evil lies close at hand. For I delight in the law of God
> in my inmost self, but I see in my members another law at war
> with the law of my mind, making me captive to the law of sin
> that dwells in my members. Wretched man that I am! Who will
> rescue me from this body of death? Thanks be to God through
> Jesus Christ our Lord! So then, with my mind I am a slave to
> the law of God, but with my flesh I am a slave to the law of
> sin. (Romans 7:15–25)

Scripture scholars remind us that this passage is not autobiograph-
ical. Rather, Paul is talking about the human condition shared by
us all. We live with divided hearts. Though our wills might desire
to serve the Master and live a life of selflessness, our selfish hearts,
often seduced by the personality props, continue to have a strong
centripetal pull. Paul deliberately uses a Greek military term, *aich-
malotizo*, "take captive," in verse 23 to imply that following the
servant leads to slavery while training the soul to walk in the footsteps of the Master leads to freedom.

Mirroring the gift and grace of the midlife transition, the first words of the two stanzas of the Peace Prayer put the centrifugal force of the spiritual life in motion. Like Abraham, Mary, Paul, Francis of Assisi, and my directee Blake, we need to renounce the personality props and gradually train our souls to look beyond ourselves. The gratuity of God's grace makes this possible, but we must respond to it. The next verses of the Peace Prayer offer practical ways of responding to grace and serving the Lord and Divine Master.

CUSTOMIZE YOUR TRAINING

- Think back to a time in your life when you heard the call of God. Did you sense it in your gut or hear it in your heart? How did you know it was from God? Did you act on it immediately, or did you spend time discerning and verifying its authenticity? In responding to it, what did you have to sacrifice?
- When do you feel the inner struggle between following the Master or the servant? What situations and people entice you to follow in the footsteps of the Master? What situations and people entice you to follow the servant?

SPIRITUAL COOLDOWN

Ponder

We do not live to ourselves, and we do not die to ourselves. If we live, we live to the Lord, and if we die, we die to the Lord; so then, whether we live or whether we die, we are the Lord's. (Romans 14:7–8)

Imitate

The devil therefore tempted [Francis] with a most severe temptation of lust. But the blessed father, as soon as he noticed it, took off his clothing and beat himself very severely with his cord, saying: "See, brother ass, thus is it becoming for you to remain, thus is it becoming for you to bear the whip. The tunic belongs to the order; stealing is not allowed. If you want to go your way, go."

But when he saw that the temptation did not leave him in spite of the scourging, even though all his members were marked with welts, he opened his cell and went out into the garden and cast himself naked into a deep pile of snow. Then gathering handfuls of snow, he made from it seven lumps like balls. And setting them before him, he began to speak to his body: "Behold," he said, "this larger one is your wife; these four are your two sons and your two daughters; the other two are your servant and your maid whom you must have to serve you. Hurry," he said, "and clothe them all, for they are dying of cold. But if caring for them in so many ways troubles you, be solicitous for serving God alone." The devil then departed quickly in confusion, and the saint returned to his cell glorifying God. (Thomas of Celano, *The Second Life of St. Francis*, 116–117)

Pray
Lord and Divine Master, may I respond to the gratuity of your grace like Abraham and Mary and thus enjoy the freedom and selflessness that come from being your servant. Amen.

CHAPTER TWO

Make Me an Instrument of Your Peace

By age twelve, after spending her early years fascinated by the life of missionaries in Bengal, Anjezë ("Agnes") Gonxhe Bojaxhiu decided she wanted to become a religious sister. In 1928, at eighteen years of age, she left her home in Albania to join the Sisters of Loreto at Loreto Abbey in Rathfarnham, Ireland. There she learned English, the language of instruction for the Sisters of Loreto, in hopes of serving in their foreign mission in India.

Agnes arrived in India in 1929 and in 1937 made her lifelong solemn vows as a Sister of Loreto. She chose to be named after Thérèse of Lisieux, the patron saint of missionaries. Not to be confused with another sister in the community who had chosen the Little Flower as her namesake, Agnes chose the Spanish spelling of the saint's name, Teresa. For almost twenty years, she taught history and geography at the Loreto convent school in Entally, eastern Calcutta, ultimately becoming its headmistress.

As a religious sister, Sister Teresa's soul training was organized around spiritual practices that no doubt motivated and helped her serve the Lord and Divine Master: daily Mass, community prayers, private meditation, personal ascetical and penitential practices, an annual retreat, and fidelity to the three vows of poverty, chastity, and obedience.

In April 1942, at the age of thirty-two, however, this Sister of Loreto would respond to the gratuity of God's grace that set the centrifugal force of her life in motion. She bound herself to a private vow, under pain of mortal sin if she broke it, "to give to God anything that He may ask—'Not to refuse Him anything.'"[10] She would respond positively to every divine request in each and every circumstance of her life, no matter how small or large, challenging or difficult. Because of this vow, she would later say, "I am a little pencil in God's hands. He does the thinking. He does the writing. He does everything and sometimes it is really hard because it is a broken pencil and He has to sharpen it a little more."[11] This stance of service became the secret to her sanctity and the source of her selflessness.

FEARS

Mother Teresa's private vow and her self-description as a pencil capture the essence of the first petition of the Peace Prayer: to become an instrument of God's peace. This kind of soul training requires not only an openness to God's grace but also the willingness to be malleable like clay and shaped by the hand of a potter (see Isaiah 64:8).

Though our prayer to be fashioned into God's instrument is a sign of our decision to follow in the footsteps of the Lord and Divine Master, we often resist the potter's fingers or—using Mother Teresa's metaphor—the sharpening that a blunt pencil requires. There are four reasons why we remain rigid and blunt.

My spiritual directee Pam is often paralyzed by *fear*. She's afraid of failure, looking foolish, and not having enough to live on. She breaks into a cold sweat when she thinks how God could radically change her life or take advantage of her generosity. "What if God stretches me beyond the limits of my ability or asks me to do the impossible? God gave us heels for one reason—so we can dig them in!"

When I tell her that God never asks the impossible of us and always supplies the necessary grace for whatever he asks, Pam turns her eyes away from me and crosses her arms and legs.

Pam is not alone. Fears also crippled and hindered Jesus from enthusiastically responding to the fingers of the potter on the Mount of Olives. Luke lets us hear his prayer, "Father, if you are willing, remove this cup from me..." (Luke 22:42). Jesus's distress and anguish were so great that "his sweat became like great drops of blood falling down on the ground" (v. 44).

Jesus's struggle gives us insight into how to handle our fears that hamper and impede not only our soul training but also our response to the gratuity of grace. We face the fears head on and allow ourselves to feel them; we don't ignore, suppress, or run from them. We voice them in the prayer of lament, "Remove this cup from me." And then, as we walk through the maze of our fears, we pray the second half of Jesus's prayer, "...not my will but yours be done" (Luke 22:42). This shifts our center of reference from ourselves to God and to his grace symbolized in the ministering angel of strength and courage (see v. 43). Openness to the divine gift of courage is the antidote for the fears that harden us to the fingers of the potter.

Attachments

Fear is not a deterrent for confident Dennis. Respected and popular with his parishioners, he was elected the president of his parish council. He also has the personality props that betray his success as a lawyer: a nice home in the suburbs, two automobiles, three expensive watches, and the latest electronic gadgets. Anyone looking from the outside would say he has everything. Anyone who knows him would say everything has him.

Dennis is like the rich young man in Mark's Gospel. He is a good man who obeys the law and keeps the commandments. But, like the rich young man, Dennis is emotionally attached to his personality props. He knows well the feeling of the rich young man who, when Jesus told him to sell his possessions and give the money to the poor in order to have treasure in heaven, "was shocked and went away grieving, for he had many possessions" (Mark 10:22).

Emotional *attachments*, especially to things like possessions, prestige, power, and popularity that we lean on for our sense of self-worth, can pose a second obstacle to the soul training of an instrument of God. They fatten us, keeping us immobile and sluggish. Sometimes expressed in our desires and expectations for certain specific outcomes—wanting to be healthy, wealthy, and wise, for example—attachments become hurdles, difficult to overcome, that impede our heart's response to grace.

How do people like the rich young man and Dennis free themselves from the grip of the personality props and overcome the hurdles of other emotional attachments? The secret is found in detachment, that grace of being indifferent to health or sickness, wealth or poverty, success or failure, a long life or a short one. Two practices help promote it. Think of them as a form of spiritual calisthenics.

The first is the daily reminder of a simple fact: things are not what they seem to be. Having more than enough, sitting on one's haunches, and daydreaming optimistically about the future makes someone a "fool"—Jesus's expression!—because no one knows what tonight will bring. Ponder the parable of the rich fool found in Luke 12:16–21 and see how it might challenge and change your illusions and delusions about current props, possessions, and other attachments.

Soul training upends the average person's understanding of success and happiness. They are not what they appear to be. This is the surprise and shock of the Beatitudes as well as the entire Sermon on the Mount (see Matthew 5–7): Jesus calls those "blessed"—the Greek word *makarios* also means "happy"— who do not have the trappings of success that Dennis enjoys but rather are poor, meek, hurting, hungry for righteousness, merciful, and persecuted. The centripetal force of the ego gradually loses its power of attraction as we allow grace to transform our thinking about external attachments, be they mental, physical, or emotional.

Detachment is aided and abetted by a second practice: Do not overidentify with anything outside yourself. Titles, labels, positions, status, rank, and occupations are rickety floorboards that can give way at any moment, exposing an unfinished basement. That certainly was my experience.

In 1992, the Franciscan Order sent out a request for volunteers to bring the Franciscan presence back to mainland China after a hiatus of more than forty years. I felt a strong, initial tug to respond since I could never remember not wanting to be a missionary to the Chinese people. However, it took me one whole year to emotionally disengage from the fame and popularity of my budding preaching career. Though I thought I had attained a sense of detachment, after about six months of living in the Far East, I went into a deep depression. I mistakenly thought it was culture shock. In fact, it was something totally different: When the fame and popularity of being a preacher were pulled from under my feet, and as I struggled to babble like a child with a new language, I realized just how attached I still was to "my" preaching career. Who exactly was I now? So much of my identity and self-worth rested on the label "preacher." It took me another year and a half to mourn the loss of my personality props and rediscover who I was without fame and popularity to lean on, prop me up, and define me. Detachment discloses the delusions of the desperate.

CONTROL

Karen reminded me of the third way we hinder our soul training as instruments of God. She was diagnosed with metastatic breast cancer. Though the prognosis looked bleak, the doctor assured her that an aggressive form of chemotherapy might offer some help and hope. Her family and friends offered incredible moral support and encouraged her to give it a try.

On the spur of the moment, Karen asked me to lead her in an intensive eight-day directed retreat. She wanted to ponder and pray and discern what was the best decision for her at sixty-eight years of age. We met once in the morning and once in the mid-afternoon for thirty minutes each. We explored the major stepping-stones of her life as well as her reflections on different Scripture passages. By the end of the fifth day, she had come to a decision. It was deepened and confirmed over the following three days.

"Father, I've had a great run. I've been happily married for forty-five years with four children and ten grandchildren. I've learned over the past twenty-five years that life gets more and more exciting the more and more I let go and surrender. That's really the secret to living life to the full. I used to live with the illusion that I was in charge. Thankfully, somewhere along the line, God saved me from myself. Deep down inside I feel so peaceful and really believe God is calling me home."

Four months later, Karen was surrounded by family and friends as she gently and peacefully handed her spirit over to God. Arriving at the hospital twenty minutes after she had died, I remembered her words, "I used to live with the illusion that I was in charge." Redeemed from the emotional need to be in control, this gentle woman had accepted her cancer as the potter's finishing touches on the masterpiece called her life.

The need to be in *control* can be such a slippery slope on the spiritual journey: When do we take charge and act? When do we hold back and trust? So many of us live delusional lives and think we're in charge not only of our lives but also of our holiness and soul training. And that is the very reason why frustration reigns supreme: We resist letting go and trusting in the fingers of the potter. We refuse to surrender. And yet, as I was reminded during those eight days of retreat with Karen, training the soul to become God's instrument occurs only in the radical act of trust. The risen Christ rightly reminded Peter, "Very truly, I tell you, when you were younger, you used to fasten your own belt and to go wherever you wished. But when you grow old, you will stretch out your hands, and someone else will fasten a belt around you and take you where you do not wish to go...Follow me" (John 21:18–19). Instruments are fashioned when we hand over control to the Lord and Divine Master and follow his lead to a place we know not where. Soul training is steeped in the gratuity of grace that is never exhausted and never expires.

A Sense of Entitlement

Terri and Traci are identical twins. Terri, the older by two minutes, is totally wrapped up in herself and has a bit of an edge to her personality. She is driven by a *sense of entitlement* that imposes unrealistic and inappropriate expectations on family and friends. Manipulative and egotistical, she is blind to the hurts, pains, and sufferings of others and insists upon her own happiness even at another's expense. Her oft-repeated mantra, "I deserve this," supports her habit of always getting what she wants.

Traci is the exact opposite—primarily because of her soul training and commitment to walking in the footsteps of the Lord and Divine Master. Committed to daily prayer, she lives with a healthy self-awareness that rightly perceives how her words and actions are received. Knowing that things change and end, she understands that life evolves and isn't always fair. She has learned the teaching of Jesus that the grain of wheat must fall to the ground and die, that is, suffering is a part of growth. Her attitude of gratitude fuels her compassion and empathy for others as well as her commitment to justice and peace. "You have to clear an interior space so God can be God. As John the Baptist said, 'He must increase, but I must decrease'" (John 3:30), she is fond of saying. Without being consciously aware of the Spirit's centrifugal force in her life, Traci has discovered that humility is the cure for her twin sister's sense of entitlement.

THE TEMPTATION IN THE DESERT

Lest we forget his humanity, Jesus himself had to confront his own fears, attachments, control issues, and sense of entitlement before he could begin his ministry. Luke's account of the temptation in the desert is not a temptation to commit a sinful act; it is a test to see if Jesus could be shaped and molded into Satan's own image.

The devil initially tempts Jesus with the fear of not having enough to eat. Jesus doesn't bite but responds, "It is written, 'One does not live by bread alone'" (Luke 4:4).

The devil then tries to seduce Jesus with the power and control of all the kingdoms of the world: "To you I will give their glory and all this authority; for it has been given over to me, and I will give it to anyone I please. If you, then, will worship me, it will all be yours" (vv. 6–7). Jesus rebuffs the allure of power.

Finally, the devil attempts to prey upon Jesus's sense of entitlement by reminding him that if he throws himself down from the pinnacle of the temple, angels will come to his beck and call. Jesus stands his ground.

The account of Jesus's temptation reveals the detachment and utter freedom Jesus possessed. The Letter to the Hebrews reminds us, "For we do not have a high priest who is unable to sympathize with our weaknesses, but we have one who in every respect has been tested as we are, yet without sin" (Hebrews 4:15). Like Jesus's, our response to being tested brings into focus the results of our soul training and highlights the fears, attachments, control issues, and sense of entitlement that betray our continuing allegiance to the servant.

Flying Trapeze Artists

Unlike Jesus, many of us are oblivious to the fears and attachments, control issues, and the sense of entitlement that jeopardize our soul training and keep us following the servant. Or worse, like Pam, Dennis, and Terri, thinking we are unable to survive without them, we deliberately cling to them. Reflecting on flying trapeze artists, Henri Nouwen aptly observed:

> Before they can be caught, they must let go. They must brave the emptiness of space.
>
> Living with this kind of willingness to let go is one of the greatest challenges we face. Whether it concerns a person, possession, or personal reputation, in so many areas we hold on at all costs. We become heroic defenders of our dearly gained happiness. We treat our sometimes inevitable losses as failures in the battle of survival.
>
> The great paradox is that it is in letting go, we receive. We find safety in unexpected places of risk. And those who try to avoid all risk, those who would try to guarantee that their hearts will not be broken, end up in a self-created hell.[12]

Whether conscious or unconscious, our tight grip on selfish attitudes, controlling behaviors, and the personality props is the bane of our soul training and lays the foundation of our self-created hell. We need to let go and "clear an interior space," to quote Traci, in order to be fashioned by grace.

Norma Jean shows us how clearing an interior space can be easily misunderstood and misinterpreted. A middle child, she feels she was never given enough attention when young. Now an adult, she has low self-esteem, rarely stands up for herself, makes light of her opinions and emotions, and spends little time making herself presentable. She justifies her attitude and behavior by telling herself this is what it means to die to oneself. Sadly, her emptiness is riddled with rancor, resentments, and regrets that find release in endless purchases of knickknacks advertised on television.

Clearing interior space does not proceed from negative feelings such as self-hatred, self-punishment, self-disgust, or self-contempt. Those feelings can only promote unhealthy patterns of behavior that eventually devolve into addictions, bad habits, and obsessions as they have in Norma Jean's life. We use things like alcohol, sex, shopping, and gambling to numb those feelings. When that happens, the interior space becomes a hoarder's nest.

Interior space is born of a positive feeling. As we open ourselves to courage, detachment, surrender, and humility—the four graces that cause our fears, attachments, need to be in control, and sense of entitlement to dissipate—we become willing to risk and brave the emptiness of space, to use Nouwen's words. Those four graces coalesce and blossom into the spirit of generous self-donation that can arise only by hanging in midair and not knowing what will happen next. At that very moment, God's instrument is fashioned.

PAUL AND KENOSIS
Unlike most of us who come to this centrifugal selflessness slowly, hesitantly, and sometimes begrudgingly, if at all, the apostle Paul

suddenly found himself called to serve the Lord and Divine Master in a rare moment of grace. This is how the Acts of the Apostles records it:

> Now as he was going along and approaching Damascus, suddenly a light from heaven flashed around him. He fell to the ground and heard a voice saying to him, "Saul, Saul, why do you persecute me?" He asked, "Who are you, Lord?" The reply came, "I am Jesus, whom you are persecuting. But get up and enter the city, and you will be told what you are to do." The men who were traveling with him stood speechless because they heard the voice but saw no one. Saul got up from the ground, and though his eyes were open, he could see nothing; so they led him by the hand and brought him into Damascus. For three days he was without sight, and neither ate nor drank (Acts 9:3–9).

Once a strict adherent to the Jewish law and a persecutor of Christians, Saul had to let go of control and a sense of entitlement, clear an interior space, and risk hanging in midair. Though we think of this passage as one of the four scriptural passages describing the conversion of the Apostle to the Gentiles (see also 1 Corinthians 15:3–8; Galatians 1:11–16; Acts 22:6–21), the Lord's words spoken to Ananias three days later suggest God wanted to use Saul in a specific way: "Go [to him], for he is an *instrument* whom I have chosen to bring my name before Gentiles and kings and before the people of Israel. I myself will show him how much he must suffer for the sake of my name" (vv. 15–16, emphasis mine). The gratuity of grace and the potter's fingers were shaping Saul into Paul.

A few years into his ministry, Paul must have come to realize that what had happened to him on the road to Damascus was, in fact, the paradigmatic action of Christ Jesus himself—and the call of everyone who walks in the footsteps of the Lord and Divine Master. He knew the Christians at Philippi were still struggling with the centripetal force of self-centeredness: they were licking their wounds inflicted from external persecution and struggling with internal divisions. Highlighting the centrifugal force of the Spirit and the need to risk letting go of whatever hampers their soul training, Paul encourages the Philippians:

> Let each of you look not to your own interests, but to the interests of others. Let the same mind be in you that was in Christ Jesus,
>   who, though he was in the form of God,
>   did not regard equality with God
>   as something to be exploited,
>   but emptied himself,
>   taking the form of a slave,
>   being born in human likeness.
> And being found in human form,
>   he humbled himself
>   and became obedient to the point of death—
>   even death on a cross (Philippians 2:4–8).

Some biblical scholars suggest this might have been an early Christian poem or an early baptismal hymn known to the Philippians. In either case, it highlights the interior space that Jesus created within himself by "emptying himself," the translation of the Greek word *kenosis*. This self-donation and outpouring of the self are the paradigmatic actions required if we are to be shaped into an instrument. Like bamboo, the more we hollow ourselves of self, the stronger we become through the gratuity of grace.

FRANCIS AND HIS FATHER

As we train our souls to confront the fears, attachments, control needs, and sense of entitlement that hinder the potter from having free rein on our lives, we discover the need to risk letting go and hanging in midair as Saul did for three days after his experience on the road to Damascus. Midair is the place where grace fashions instruments of God. Saint Francis provides another example of this exercise in soul training.

Once released from prison and having dreamt that God was asking him to serve the Master and not the servant, Francis had to confront the personality props that still held a grip on his heart. It would be a dramatic moment of letting go.

Francis's father felt shamed by the antics of his son: prodigally distributing his hard-earned money to the poor and ministering to the lepers who lived outside the walls of Assisi. The future saint's actions betray the tension between the centripetal and centrifugal forces in his own life: Francis's generosity required his father's money. He looked beyond himself to care for the marginalized of his day. Demanding that both behaviors stop immediately, his father demanded a public audience with the bishop of Assisi who alone held the right to arbiter disputes with those dedicated to the Lord and Divine Master.

The parties assembled in the square in front of the cathedral of San Rufino. Francis's father aired his frustration and grievance. Bishop Guido told Francis he had to give back the money he had taken from his father. The idea of returning his father's money no doubt stung Francis's sense of entitlement. In a rare moment of one-upmanship and no doubt responding to the gratuity of grace, Francis declared, "I will not only return the money to my father but also my clothes." Stripping before all and laying both the money and his clothes at the feet of his father, Francis declared,

"Up until now I have called Pietro Bernardone my father, but now I say, 'Our Father who art in heaven.'" It was Francis's own moment of clearing an interior space, of letting go, of emptying himself, and hanging in midair. The soul training, fashioning him into an instrument, continued.

THE GIFT OF THE RISEN LORD

What was Francis's mission as an instrument of God? What was the message God wanted to proclaim with his life? It was fundamentally the mission and message that we all share: the mission and message of the risen Christ.

The first words of the risen Lord to his disciples are his greeting and his gift, "Peace be with you" (John 20:19). This Easter peace, won at the price of Jesus's own self-emptying in his birth and death, was such a precious gift that Paul referred to it with this distinctive greeting: "Grace to you and peace from God our Father and the Lord Jesus Christ" (Romans 1:7; see also 1 Corinthians 1:3; Galatians 1:3; Philippians 1:2). In a world that was considering Christianity more and more subversive, the disciples were reminded that the *kenosis* of the Lord and Divine Master—and any faithful servant of his, for that matter—was a portal of peace for others.

The early Christians transformed this gift into a lifestyle. For the first three hundred years of Christianity, followers of Christ refused to participate in battles. They believed the Lord's peace could not be reconciled with bearing arms in war. To follow the Prince of Peace meant fostering the politics of peace.

But how does one foster the politics of peace? Certainly, it must mean more than the absence of anger, bitterness, and hostilities. The following six petitions of the Peace Prayer suggest the legacy of peace must seep deep down and eradicate the very reactions that point to the centripetal force in one's life: hatred, injury, doubt, despair, darkness, and sadness.

Kay is one of those people who remembers every injury and hurt she has ever experienced. Mention a person's name to her, and she can rattle off a litany of past slights and affronts. She has built up so much anger, bitterness, and resentment that even the slightest misstep can cause her to explode with anger. She mopes through each day and is suspicious of virtually everyone. She often sits alone at night drinking heavily and wondering why no one gives her the appropriate respect she thinks she deserves.

The Peace Prayer indicates that if we spend a lot of time in front of the mirror staring at ourselves, we will never enjoy peace. Like Kay, we will continue to be chained to our fears, attachments, control issues, and sense of entitlement. Or we will go through each day seething with resentment. Or, even worse, we will constantly be throwing a pity party and feeling very much alone and isolated. Following the example of the Lord and Divine Master, Paul, and Saint Francis, we too must clear an interior space and empty ourselves for peace to blossom within our lives and the lives of others.

Peacemaking

Clearing the interior space means being a peacekeeper whose soul is trained to look beyond itself. Jesus says, "But I say to you, Do not resist an evildoer. But if anyone strikes you on the right cheek, turn the other also" (Matthew 5:39). Following in the footsteps of the Lord and Divine Master to Calvary and imitating his example on the cross, we absorb the violence and pain inflicted upon us. We refuse to continue the vicious, violent cycle of striking back, retaliating, or seeking revenge. In doing so, the selfless centrifugal force is activated as our internal pain becomes a tributary of external peace for others.

However, becoming a tributary for others is not simply a matter of holding my tongue and renouncing the temptation to strike back and seek revenge. I must become a field hand—an active agent—who intentionally sows the seeds of peace for others.

As a peacemaker for others, I take a prophetic stand by committing myself to uprooting any source of hatred, injury, despair, sadness, or darkness that other people endure. I stand up and speak out against any form of prejudice, discrimination, or injustice. Though I might speak with the anger of a prophet, I never use or incite violence when working for peace. God's peace is never bequeathed through a clenched fist or proclaimed through the barrel of a pistol.

My goal is not to manhandle my neighbors and force them to change. Rather, my words, actions, and lifestyle should compel others to take a second or third look at their own personal attitudes or the societal structures that oppress or exploit the weaker and disenfranchised members of society. This reexamination of attitudes and structures can cause a conversation and the dawning of justice as people move from selfishness to selflessness. Indeed, peace can never fully blossom in a world where there is no justice. Sowing the seeds of peace means first tilling the ground for justice.

INSPIRATION DAY

More than four years after making her private vow, Sister Teresa was taking the train from Calcutta to Darjeeling. She was going for her annual retreat followed by a period of rest and relaxation. At some point during that twenty-one-hour trip, she had a mystical experience of Jesus. Though she never spoke about the details of the experience, she once revealed how she interpreted it:

> [It] was a call within my vocation. It was a second calling. It
> was a vocation to give up even Loreto where I was very happy

and to go out in the streets to serve the poorest of the poor. It was in that train, I heard the call to give up all and follow Him into the slums—to serve Him in the poorest of the poor...I knew it was His will and that I had to follow Him. There was no doubt that it was going to be His work.[13]

She would later refer to September 10, 1946, as her "Inspiration Day." Because her vow of obedience required her to secure the necessary permissions from both the archbishop of Calcutta and the religious superior of the Sisters of Loreto, she was unable to fulfill her private vow immediately. That frustrated her deeply. However, on August 17, 1948, clad in a white sari with a blue border and with only five rupees (the equivalent of less than four dollars at the time) in her pocket, the future Saint Mother Teresa of Calcutta went into the slums and, using her metaphor of a pencil, began to write God's love letter to the poorest of the poor.

Mother Teresa wasn't the only one to be inspired by God to become an instrument of peace. Frank's inspiration came one afternoon when he discovered a homeless community living under a bridge. For the next eighteen years, he donated his time and money to a soup kitchen in Chicago. God currently uses Suzanne, the wife of an ambassador in Beijing, who sells her artwork and then contributes the money earned to an orphanage for children with special needs. God calls Justin to make quarterly visits to the southern border of the United States to bring provisions, peace, and hope to those in detention centers. Like Mother Teresa, Lisa is also God's pencil as she maintains a pen-pal relationship with an inmate on death row. God inspires Aaron, a lawyer by profession, to accept pro bono cases on behalf of inner-city apartment tenants and, consequently, to single-handedly change the living conditions of a section of Seattle.

Such responses speak volumes about the true meaning of social justice. It is not merely about doing good or being a philanthropist. It goes beyond simply standing up for humanitarian concerns. Rather, social justice is creating opportunities for every person to live life fully in the here and now. Attained through the lives of Christ and his instruments, such opportunities form the roots that nourish the gift of peace.

The Peace Prayer envisions us as farmers in the world. Like our Divine Master, we create an interior space by emptying ourselves of fears, attachments, control issues, and the sense of entitlement. We look beyond the pain others inflict upon us and refuse to strike back in violence. Indeed, we beat the swords of our hearts into plowshares and the spears of our souls into pruning hooks (see Isaiah 2:4). As instruments, we then ask for the grace to actively till the earth and sow the seeds of peace while waiting with great anticipation for the harvest of justice.

....

CUSTOMIZE YOUR TRAINING

- Name the fears that tighten and constrict your heart. What are the attachments that weigh you down and hinder you from serving the Lord and Divine Master? What frustrations in your life are the result of your obsession to remain in control? In what ways does a sense of entitlement impede you from letting go and hanging in midair?
- When did you experience an "Inspiration Day"? What were the circumstances? How did you respond to that grace from God? How have you been faithful or unfaithful to that grace?

....

SPIRITUAL COOLDOWN

Ponder

In a large house there are utensils not only of gold and silver but also of wood and clay, some for special use, some for ordinary. All who cleanse themselves of the things I have mentioned will become special utensils, dedicated and useful to the owner of the house, ready for every good work. (2 Timothy 2:20–21)

Imitate

Look at God's condescension, my brothers, and pour out your hearts before him (Psalm 61:9). Humble yourselves that you may be exalted by him (cf. 1 Peter 5:6). Keep nothing for yourselves, so that he who has given himself wholly to you may receive you wholly. (Francis of Assisi, "A Letter to a General Chapter")

Pray

Lord and Divine Master, may your grace reveal the obstacles I put in your way. After removing them, may I then be fashioned into an instrument of your peace. Amen.

....

Where There Is Hatred, Let Me Sow Love

According to chapter twenty-one of the fourteenth-century *Little Flowers of Saint Francis*, the townspeople of Gubbio were being terrorized by a big, fearsome, and ferocious wolf who devoured not only the local animals but also the citizens themselves. Fear of the beast so consumed the people that when they went outside the city walls, they would arm themselves as if going to battle. Those who traveled alone and encountered the beast never returned home. The situation escalated to such an extent that no one dared to go outside the city walls.

While staying in Gubbio, Saint Francis heard about the plight of the citizens. Against everyone's advice, he decided to confront the wolf. Making the sign of the cross and putting his trust in God, Francis, accompanied by some brothers and townspeople, walked outside the city gates and followed the road leading to the wolf's den. The wolf, seeing the crowd coming into his territory, charged at the saint with mouth wide open. Making the sign of the cross over the animal, Francis ordered, "Brother Wolf, I command you in the name of Christ, don't!" The wolf immediately closed his mouth, stopped running, and, like a gentle lamb, plopped himself at the feet of the saint.

"Brother Wolf, you have done such terrible things—even going so far as to kill people who are made in the image of God," said the saint, speaking the truth in love. "You deserve the gallows. All the citizens of Gubbio complain about you and have become your enemy. But I want to make peace between you and them. If you stop offending them, they will forgive your offenses and stop persecuting you. Do you agree?"

The wolf showed his acceptance by moving his body, tail, and ears and bowing his head.

"I understand very well," continued Francis, "that you did these terrible deeds out of hunger. Since you are willing to make this pact, I promise you: you will be fed every day if you promise not to hurt the animals or the townspeople again. Do you promise?"

The wolf made a sign to show his promise.

"Brother Wolf, I want you to guarantee this promise so I can trust it." Saint Francis held out his hand, and the wolf lifted his right paw and tamely placed it in the saint's hand. The deal was struck.

"Brother Wolf, I command you in the name of Christ to come with me so we can seal this peace pact in the name of God."

The saint and the wolf made their way inside the city gates to the piazza. Once all the townspeople assembled, Francis preached a short sermon encouraging Gubbio's citizens to turn from their sins and reminding them that the flames of hell, lasting forever for the damned, are more dangerous than the fierceness of a wolf who can kill only the body.

Having finished preaching, Saint Francis publicly stated the terms of peace agreed to by the wolf. And he once again asked for a public display of the wolf's agreement and guarantee. Seeing all of this, the townspeople gave praise and thanks to God for sending the saint to them and, through his merits, freeing them from the jaws of the cruel beast.

The wolf lived peacefully for two more years within the city walls of Gubbio. He received food daily as he went from door to door. He no longer harmed anyone and gradually won the hearts of all the citizens who grieved very much over his death.

Though this quaint story reads like a child's fairy tale, some scholars have suggested a historical basis for it. In 1873, while renovating the Chiesa di San Francesco della Pace (Church of Saint Francis of the Peace), located near the place where the peace pact supposedly took place, workers found a cross-emblazoned stone, dating from the early Middle Ages, that covered a sarcophagus containing the skeleton of an animal confirmed by a municipal veterinarian to be a wolf; it was transferred and buried in the crypt of the renovated church. The church's website currently notes: "Local popular tradition also referred to that site as being the burial place of the Wolf tamed by St. Francis, a fact further supported by the ancient toponomastic designation of the spot under the name 'Trivio Morlupi,' or Morlupi crossroads (Latin *mors lupi*: the death of the wolf)."[14]

Other scholars have suggested that what came to be symbolized in the wolf originally was a roaming bandit terrorizing Gubbio. Whether fact or fiction, the story portrays a disciple of the Lord and Divine Master who knew that peace is possible only when you sow love amid hatred.

The Logistics of Love

Love is the preeminent sign that one walks in the footsteps of the Lord and Divine Master: "By this everyone will know that you are my disciples, if you have love for one another" (John 13:35). The story of the wolf of Gubbio offers some practical exercises to train the soul in the logistics of love so that peace can be restored and preserved.[15]

Be yourself. Soul training in love begins with the acknowledgment that we are all brothers and sisters with the same heavenly Father. Our familial ties form the foundation of God's kingdom on earth. Knowing instinctively the connection he shared with the beast, Francis continually addressed the wolf as "Brother Wolf." All relationships—and negotiations—start on a level playing field where mutual respect reigns and where we refuse the temptation to condemn or demoralize the other with the title "enemy." Harsh, angry, bitter, or malicious words sometimes betray fears, as well as a sense of superiority and entitlement.

Be other-centered. Soul training in love continues as we activate the centrifugal force in our lives: we shift the point of reference from ourselves to the other. This requires the willingness to get involved, reach out, and encounter the other as Francis did with the wolf. Loving from afar is the stuff of fantasy and infatuation.

Be vulnerable. Knowing that conflicts arise from unjust situations, we make the journey toward the other unarmed and undefended. Anger, vindictiveness, revenge, and the need to be proven right are all weapons that escalate the situation. Francis walked the path to the wolf with only the sign of the cross—the very symbol of nonviolent vulnerability and the renunciation of vengeance, retaliation, and reprisal; indeed, its only demand is forgiveness: "Father, forgive them; for they do not know what they are doing" (Luke 23:34).

Be compassionate. Knowing instinctively that all love resides in compassion, Francis put himself in the shoes of the wolf and tried to understand the animal's reactions. This highlights the truest meaning of compassion not as sympathy or solace but as "suffering with" (from the Latin *cum* meaning "with" and *passio* meaning "to suffer"). This step revealed that the wolf's violence arose from an unmet basic need: "I understand very well that you did these terrible deeds out of hunger." Lack of food had to be addressed for peace to reign.

Be the catalyst for justice and social change. Love never flinches from ensuring basic rights; that's the essence of justice that leads to lasting peace. That guarantee can happen only when structures in society promote a level playing field for everyone. Knowing that, Francis convinced the citizens of Gubbio to feed the wolf every day. With the basic right to have food satisfied by that material expression of charity, peace returned to a city ravaged by fear and death.

NOT A FEELING OR EMOTION

We often think of love as the tenderness, warmth, deep affection, or devotion for another expressed in innumerable physical ways: a hammering heart, a racing pulse, butterflies in the stomach, a soulful glow, a gleeful glance across the room, wanting to lean in and touch the other, getting tongue-tangled, or obsessively checking for text messages from the beloved. The story of the taming of Gubbio's wolf, however, suggests the nature of love that leads to peace is something very different. It begins with a commitment to self-knowledge: I know who I am vis-à-vis the other person; I am a member of the same family. It continues with the decision to detach from the ego with its fears, need for attachments and control, and its sense of entitlement. I clear an interior space and focus my attention on the other. It matures into a fearless vulnerability that is willing courageously to confront the other without cruelty and brutality. It is the promise and pledge to put myself in the other's shoes, experience the same situation, and then have it resolved with the appropriate social changes that ensure justice for all. No wonder Paul writes, "And now faith, hope, and love abide, these three; and the greatest of these is love" (1 Corinthians 13:13).

PAUL'S DESCRIPTION

The Apostle to the Gentiles affirms that love is more of an intentional dedication and willful commitment than a supersized feeling or a gushing emotion. To the church in Corinth, torn by various factions that were vying for a sense of superiority, recognition, and prestige, Paul wrote that love must be the basic and preeminent foundation of any person or community claiming to have spiritual gifts: without it, "I am a resounding gong or a clashing cymbal...I am nothing...I gain nothing." (1 Corinthians 13:1–3). Using fifteen Greek verbs—highlighting the dynamism of his understanding of love—that are translated as adjectives in English, he described the centrifugal dedication and commitment that move a believer to his understanding of love. His description makes for an excellent examination of conscience to determine if my soul training is leading me to walk in the footsteps of the Lord and Divine Master.

Love is patient (v. 4). How do I demonstrate my perseverance, persistence, and tenacity in relationships? Who or what situations make me irritable, frustrated, or annoyed?

Love is kind (v. 4). What practices help me to move from selfishness to selflessness? How do I express my care, concern, and consideration for others as Saint Francis did both with the citizens of Gubbio and its wolf?

Love is not jealous (v. 4). How often do I compare myself to other people? When does the green-eyed monster rear its head and make me feel resentful and bitter?

Love is not pompous; it is not inflated (v. 4). What groups of people or situations spark my sense of entitlement? When am I domineering and overbearing? How do I follow Saint Francis's example and express my familial ties with those who are difficult and testy?

Love is not rude (v. 5). To whom am I consistently ill-mannered, impolite, and discourteous? Why?

Love does not seek its own interests (v. 5). How often do I hear myself say or think "I need," "I deserve," "I want"? What attachments control me? In what areas of my life do I insist on being in control? What activates a sense of entitlement in me?

Love is not quick-tempered (v. 5). When do I feel the need to be abrasive or hurtful like the wolf of Gubbio? Who irritates and annoys me? Why?

Love does not brood over injury (v. 5). When am I tempted to lick my wounds? When am I attached to self-pity and want to feel sorry for myself?

Love does not rejoice over wrongdoing but rejoices with the truth (v. 6). Like Saint Francis confronting the wolf, how do I speak the truth in love? In what situations do I hesitate to speak up and call a spade a spade? Why?

Love bears all things, believes all things, hopes all things, endures all things (v. 7). How do I hold and honor my hurts, sorrows, and injuries? How do I sustain and support familial ties with people who have treated me unjustly? How can my heart be converted to compassion and understanding as were the hearts of Gubbio's townspeople?

Prisoner 16670

This examination of conscience helps to broaden our awareness of those areas where both the ego's centripetal force is still active and our soul training needs to be intensified. As our self-awareness deepens and we actively clear an interior space by exercising the other-centered virtues of patience, kindness, humility, selflessness, and compassion, we find our hearts expanding and our familial ties with others strengthening. At times this spontaneously blossoms into the kenotic selflessness of Christ on the cross: "We know love by this, that he laid down his life for us—and we ought to lay down our lives for one another" (1 John 3:16). We see this so clearly in the life of Prisoner 16670 of Auschwitz.

At twelve years of age, Rajmund Kolbe had a vision of the Blessed Virgin that would begin his soul training: When he asked the Mother of God what was to become of him in life, she appeared, carrying a white crown and a red crown. Mary asked him if he would be willing to accept one of these crowns. He would later explain in his own words, "The white one meant that I should persevere in purity and the red that I should become a martyr. I said that I would accept them both."[16] Four years later, in 1910, he entered the Conventual Franciscan Order and was given the religious name Maximilian. As a friar, he was ordained a priest, received a doctorate in philosophy, founded a few publications and an amateur radio station, and promoted devotion to the Immaculate Virgin Mary as a way to convert sinners and enemies of the Catholic Church. Between 1930 and 1936, he undertook missions to China, Japan, and India.

Poor health forced him to return to his native Poland in 1936 where he and a few remaining friars ran a temporary hospital in the friary. He was arrested and imprisoned by the Germans during the final four months of 1939. Upon his release, he and the friars began providing shelter for three thousand Polish refugees, two-thirds of whom were Jews, displaced and threatened by war. One can see the centrifugal force active in his life as he shared housing, food, and clothing with these people while telling the friars, "We must do everything in our power to help these unfortunate people who have been driven from their homes and deprived of even the most basic necessities. Our mission is among them in the days that lie ahead."[17] On February 17, 1941, the friary was shut down by the German Gestapo, and Kolbe was taken prisoner. After three months in a German-occupied Warsaw prison, he was transferred to Auschwitz.

Arriving at the concentration camp, he immediately was put to work carrying blocks of stone for the construction of a crematorium wall. He was taunted and harassed both for his faith and his priesthood. He was beaten to the point of death, revived, and then sent to the infirmary bunker where he encouraged the sick to pray for the very people they hated, their Nazi captors.

In late July or early August 1941, a prisoner of Block 11 escaped from Auschwitz. As a punishment, ten prisoners were handpicked from the same barracks to die of starvation. The last prisoner selected, Polish sergeant Francis Gajowniczek, let out a cry that he was married with children. At that moment, spontaneously putting himself in the sergeant's shoes, Kolbe stepped forward and volunteered to take his place. When the *SS-Hauptsturmfürer* asked who he was, Kolbe replied, "I am a Catholic priest. I wish to die for that man. I am old, he has a wife and children."[18] In the face of Nazi Germany's hatred for Jews and Catholics, Maximilian Kolbe sowed a seed of love with his very life.

Kolbe and the nine other prisoners went to a slow death by torture and starvation in Block 13. After three weeks, only he and three others were still alive—and barely at that. On August 14, to hasten their deaths, the commandant ordered that they be injected with carbonic acid. Their corpses were sent immediately to the crematorium.

Pope Paul VI beatified Kolbe in 1971 and called him "that martyr of charity."[19] Eleven years later, in his homily for Kolbe's canonization, his Polish compatriot, Pope John Paul II, highlighted the sacrificial love shown by Kolbe: "He spontaneously offered himself up to death out of love. And in this human death of his there was the clear witness borne to Christ: the witness borne in Christ to the dignity of man, to the sanctity of life, and to the saving power of death in which the power of love is made manifest."[20]

For fifty years after his liberation from the concentration camp, Gajowniczek made an annual pilgrimage back to Auschwitz on August 14 to honor the man and the love that blossomed amid Nazi hatred.

The same love sown amid hatred that motivated Saint Maximilian Kolbe also motivates ordinary people and organizations. Pete Carrol, head coach of the NFL's Seattle Seahawks, founded A Better LA, a nonprofit organization in Los Angeles that supports community-based solutions to bridge racial divides, creates safer neighborhoods for children and families, and links individuals in the inner city to resources they need to thrive. Marge, a Human Resources director in a large corporation, has a firm commitment and track record not only for resolving conflicts among employees, but also for addressing gossip and hearsay that sow distrust and dislike among coworkers. Started in 1991 after a tragic drive-by shooting of a Denver teen, GRASP (Gang Rescue and Support Project) is a peer-run intervention program of ex-gang members that helps at-risk youth or those wanting to leave gangs. Reed, a spiritual directee, is never afraid to speak up and lovingly confront any form of prejudice or discrimination among his family and friends. In the aftermath of World War II, two Frenchmen, Marthe Dortel-Claudot and Bishop Pierre-Marie Théas, were inspired to start Pax Christi International, an organization initially aimed at reconciling French and German citizens; now with 120 member organizations, it promotes "peace, respect of human rights, justice and reconciliation throughout the world."[21] Begun in 1961 when two Portuguese students were jailed for raising a toast to freedom, Amnesty International protects people wherever justice, freedom, truth, and dignity are denied. These people and organizations and hundreds like them, each in its own way, are sowing seeds of love amid ill feeling, hostility, hatred, and enmity.

The Roots of Hatred

Organizations like A Better LA, GRASP, Pax Christi International, and Amnesty International exist because hatred and injustice are present in the world. People like Marge and Reed make us aware how distrust and prejudice creep into boardrooms, bedrooms, and living rooms. But why?

The fourth chapter of the book of Genesis gives us one explanation for hatred. Though brothers, Cain and Abel had different occupations: Cain was a shepherd, Abel a farmer. Genesis suggests the source of Cain's hatred for his younger brother: "In the course of time Cain brought to the Lord an offering of the fruit of the ground, and Abel for his part brought of the firstlings of his flock, their fat portions. And the Lord had regard for Abel and his offering, but for Cain and his offering he had no regard. So Cain was very angry, and his countenance fell" (Genesis 4:3–5). Anger born of envy or jealousy is one source of our dislike and hatred for others.

How tempting it is to view life as a competition and others as our competitors. I see it in myself when I hear of people who are receiving accolades for their speaking or writing ability. I instantly want to disparage their accomplishment or sully their reputation. Envy at someone's natural gift or jealousy over someone's possessions has a way of morphing into hatred, malice—and, in Cain's case, murder.

Hatred can also be taught by stereotypes and biases based on historical animosities. While teaching in mainland China in the late 1990s, I always raised an eyebrow over my college students' intense loathing and hatred for the Japanese. I quickly learned that twice a month they were subjected to "political education" and reminded time and again about the December 1937 to January 1938 Nanjing Massacre, the six-week mass murder and rape committed by Imperial Japanese troops against the residents of the then-capital of China during the Second Sino-Japanese War. Strangely, the instructors of the political education classes were in their late thirties and themselves had been taught this national prejudice by a previous generation of educators.

Of course, one doesn't need to go to Asia to discover how people are educated to be intolerant and aggressive. Nationalized bigotry and prejudice were the beating hearts of Nazi Germany and apartheid South Africa. Neo-Nazi skinheads and the Ku Klux Klan in the United States are often encouraged by their own to promote madness, mayhem, and even murder. They are aided and abetted by more than a thousand hate-mongering websites that disseminate their false, distorted, and bigoted information.

Ignorance and fear are two more sources of our hatred. We are often uncomfortable with people whom we perceive to be different from us. Because of their race, religion, culture, sexual orientation, or some other superficial difference, we tend to polarize and divide the world into "us" and "them." This is the essence of xenophobia, the fear, distrust, and even hatred of anything considered strange and foreign. This divide can be exacerbated if we have an unpleasant encounter with one of "them"; we immediately presume "they" are all like that. As a Catholic priest in the early 2000s, I often saw parents instinctively hover over their children in a protective stance when they saw a man wearing a Roman collar. If someone is immature and lacks a backbone, that person might seek out like-minded individuals to strengthen this "us" and "them" polarization; this can devolve into a mob mentality or group bullying.

It's not just our differences that sometimes give rise to bad blood and hostility. Our similarities can also give rise to resentment and distrust as we project what we dislike about ourselves onto those who might be like us. Benedict, for example, refuses to face the consequences of his inappropriate angry reactions and claims his brother has an anger management problem. Julie is crushed by the feeling of an emotional void in her marriage yet constantly complains that nothing makes her husband content.

History has also shown how antagonism, acrimony, and enmity can be justified in the name of religion. The Middle Ages gave rise to the crusades and the inquisition. Early Modern Europe and North America had their witch hunts. In the beginning of the 1990s, the Sikhs rose up in violence against the Muslims in India; Serbian Orthodox Christians attacked Croatian Catholics and Bosnian Muslims in the former Yugoslavia; Muslim extremists demanded the imposition of Islamic law in Africa and the Middle East; Catholics and Protestants continued their fighting in Northern Ireland; Hindus and Buddhists clashed in Sri Lanka.

A COUNTERCULTURAL RESPONSE

It's in such a chaotic, violent world that the Lord and Divine Master's clarion call still rings:

> You have heard that it was said, "An eye for an eye and a tooth for a tooth." But I say to you, Do not resist an evildoer. But if anyone strikes you on the right cheek, turn the other also... You have heard that it was said, "You shall love your neighbor and hate your enemy." But I say to you, Love your enemies and pray for those who persecute you, so that you may be children

of your Father in heaven; for he makes his sun rise on the evil
and on the good, and sends rain on the righteous and on the
unrighteous. For if you love those who love you, what reward
do you have? Do not even the tax collectors do the same? And
if you greet only your brothers and sisters, what more are you
doing than others? Do not even the Gentiles do the same? Be
perfect, therefore, as your heavenly Father is perfect. (Matthew
5:38–39, 43–48)

Serving the Lord and Divine Master requires the practice of a
whole new routine in soul training: a nonviolent reaction and
response that seeks no retaliation to aggression and hostility, an
openness to all people despite how they might have treated us.
This is the practical and countercultural consequence when one
commits to love.

Jewish law, as enshrined in chapter twenty-four of the book of
Leviticus, not only allowed but also called for proportionate resti-
tution: "Anyone who kills a human being shall be put to death...
Anyone who maims another shall suffer the same injury in return:
fracture for fracture, eye for eye, tooth for tooth; the injury
inflicted is the injury to be suffered" (Leviticus 24:17, 19–20; see
also Exodus 21:24; Deuteronomy 19:21). The law intended to
strictly limit the spiral of violence. With his teaching, Jesus over-
turns and nullifies this ancient law. The disciple does not respond
in kind but rather sows the seed of love when confronted with
hateful, aggressive, and even mortal actions.

But Jesus doesn't stop there. He goes further. The Torah clearly
states, "You shall not take vengeance or bear a grudge against
any of your people, but you shall love your neighbor as yourself: I am the Lord" (Leviticus 19:18), suggesting the common
understanding that one's neighbor meant one's fellow coun-
tryman. It mentioned nothing about the enemy. Jesus, however,

quotes another statement, "You shall love your neighbor and hate your enemy" (Matthew 5:43), perhaps referring to a contemporary Pharisaical interpretation of the Levitical law. Jesus not only challenges that interpretation, but also explicitly commands love and prayers for the enemy and the persecutor. Those who follow in the footsteps of the Lord and Divine Master have hearts like the Father: open to all, the good and the evil, the righteous and the unrighteous, the tax collector and the Gentile. This is what it means to imitate the Father's perfection (Luke 6:36 speaks of mercy instead of perfection) and to mirror the familial relationship shared by all.

THE SAINT AND THE SULTAN

Another incident in the life of Saint Francis provides an excellent example of loving the enemy. Francis's encounter with the sultan around September 1219, documented nine times within the first fifteen years after it took place, reveals love being sown amid religious hatred and conflict.

During the Fifth Crusade, while sieging the city of Damietta, Egypt, located at the mouth of the Nile, the Crusaders undertook an aggressive assault on the Muslim army. This resulted in a devastating Christian defeat and a brief truce. During that lull in the fighting, Francis and Brother Illuminato arrived in the Christian camp with the hope of negotiating peace between the Christian Crusaders and the Muslim sultan. The two convinced Cardinal Pelagius, the papal legate who was blocking peace negotiations, to permit them to cross the battle lines and engage Sultan Malik al-Kamil at his court. Historians are uncertain how long Francis and his companion stayed in the Muslim camp, but, after what could have been as many as three weeks, the two were given safe passage to return to the Christian camp. Francis left Egypt shortly thereafter and returned to Assisi.

We do not know what the saint and the sultan discussed, but the fact that the two friars were allowed to remain among the Muslims for several days speaks eloquently of the sultan's hospitality and the harmony arising among the three. Presumably Francis and Illuminato witnessed to the Abba revealed in the person of Jesus while al-Kamil and his court witnessed to Allah as revealed in the Quran of Muhammad.

Though we do not know what was discussed, we do know the conversations' effect on each. In the revised Rule of 1221, Francis wrote that the friars who want to go among the Muslims should not quarrel with them or cause them disputes but should live among them "spiritually," "be subject to every human creature for God's sake (1 Peter 2:13)," and to acknowledge that they are Christians.[22] His *Praises of God*, reminiscent of the Muslim *Ninety-Nine Beautiful Names of God*, might have been influenced by his experience and discussions with the sultan. The suggestion in his *Letter to the Rulers of the People* that mayors, consuls, magistrates, and governors have a messenger formally announce a prayer time in the evening might have arisen from his experience of the *sâlat*, the Islamic call to prayer announced five times a day.

After flooding the Christian camp with the waters of the Nile and engulfing the Crusaders in mud, Sultan Malik al-Kamil allowed the incapacitated soldiers to surrender peacefully rather than having them massacred. He sent them daily bread for survival until they could leave Egypt unharmed. The Christians, touched by such mercy and compassion, believed that the sultan had been baptized secretly. He wasn't. Perhaps al-Kamil had been influenced by his time with Saint Francis or simply was following in the footsteps of his uncle Saladin who was known for his friendship with Egyptian Christians.

A town, a wolf, and a mutual agreement among brothers. A Jew, a Catholic, and an extraordinary step of fraternal compassion. Ordinary people and organizations working for a safe and just world. A sultan, a saint, and an early attempt at interreligious dialogue. When disciples of the Lord and Divine Master seek to console, understand, and love one another as members of the same family in times of hatred, they exhibit the finest soul training and sow the seeds of peace in the furrows of the world.

CUSTOMIZE YOUR TRAINING

- Spend an hour examining your conscience based upon Paul's description of love. In what aspects of love have you been well trained? In what aspects do you need to intensify your soul training?
- This chapter mentioned six sources of hatred: jealousy, education by stereotype and historical bias, ignorance, fear, projection of similarities on others, and religious fanaticism. What are other sources? How have you experienced these sources in your own life?

SPIRITUAL COOLDOWN

Ponder

Those who say, "I love God," and hate their brothers or sisters, are liars; for those who do not love a brother or sister whom they have seen, cannot love God whom they have not seen. The commandment we have from him is this: those who love God must love their brothers and sisters also. (1 John 4:20–21)

Imitate

Remember the words of our Lord, Love your enemies, do good to those who hate you (Mt. 5:44). Our Lord Jesus Christ himself, in whose footsteps we must follow (cf. 1 Peter 2:21), called the man who betrayed him his friend, and gave himself up of his own accord to his executioners. Therefore, our friends are those who for no reason cause us trouble and suffering, shame or injury, pain or torture, even martyrdom and death. It is these we must love, and love very much, because for all they do to us we are given eternal life. (Francis of Assisi, "The Rule of 1221")

Pray
Lord and Divine Master, may your grace challenge me to move from selfishness to selflessness and to make the commitment to love my neighbor as myself. Amen.

....

CHAPTER FOUR

Where There Is Injury, Pardon; It Is in Pardoning that We Are Pardoned

The opening song of the funeral liturgy was about to begin. Though I tried my best to be present to my relatives and the friends who had gathered, I was once again replaying in my head what had happened thirty-four years earlier. That incident led me to be in the church this day for my aunt's funeral.

It happened on my vacation in June 1981 as I introduced another friar to the sights and sounds of my hometown, New Orleans. We boarded the St. Charles Avenue streetcar at the beginning of the line and then rolled down Carrollton Avenue. To this day, I still don't know what possessed me to get off the streetcar at the Oak Street stop. But we did.

I had not walked down Oak Street since my father's suicide in 1968. But even after thirteen years, so much of it remained the same. The big blue and white sign still proclaimed, "Haase's Shoe Store." I remembered being ten, eleven, and twelve years old and taking the St. Charles streetcar to Oak Street to surprise my father with a visit after school. I remembered how my father would take me into his office that overlooked the sales area of the store. I remembered the pet parakeet and how I would spend endless hours trying to get that bird to say, "Welcome to Haase's."

I had not been in the store since my father's funeral. At the news of his sudden and tragic death, each side of the family pointed a finger of blame at the other. As a result, I had not seen my father's side of the family or the shoe store for thirteen years. My father's sister, my aunt Vera May, now owned and managed the shoe store. As my friend and I passed the store, I suddenly felt drawn to go in. I was scared. I had not seen my aunt for more than a decade. And frankly, I did not know if I wanted to see her now. But within a matter of seconds, I found myself inside my father's store. A salesman, later revealed to be one of my cousins, approached and asked if he could help me.

I must have looked foolish. I just stood there and finally blurted out, "Is Vera May here?"

Within a few minutes, I heard steps coming down the stairs from my father's office. There she stood. Aunt Vera May.

We stared at each other: she, probably trying to figure out who I was, and I, gazing upon a face so familiar that I thought my father had suddenly come alive.

Within in a split second, she recognized me. And with that, the gift was given instantly. It was the blossom of two broken hearts. Pardon. Forgiveness. Reconciliation.

For the first time in thirteen years, my aunt and I embraced, shed tears of sorrow and regret, and held each other. It was then that I discovered something that I should have known all along. The pain of my father's death, which had consumed me for all those years, was just as real for my aunt. She too had loved my father. I discovered then and there the ugliness and lie of holding grudges. They strip the other person of a human heart.

My friend Dan just stood there. When it finally dawned on him what he had just witnessed, he signed himself with the cross. And maybe that is the best response to a moment of forgiveness: to call to mind the crucified Christ who forgave his own persecutors as he hung upon the cross.

THE ART AND HEART OF FORGIVENESS

Forgiveness makes a lot of practical sense, doesn't it? It takes a lot of emotional energy to keep a grudge alive, to stoke the fires of resentment, to hang on to a hurt. According to the Mayo Clinic's website, people who nurse anger, harbor animosity, and refuse to forgive bring these negative emotions into every relationship and new experience, thus experiencing people and events through a distorted filter. Some people become so absorbed in their injury that they are blind and deaf to the sights and sounds of the present moment. Others sometimes numb their depression or rage with unhealthy compulsive behavior centered on sex, alcohol, shopping, or gambling. Still others feel that life has lost its sparkle all the while feeling at odds with their spiritual beliefs. Sometimes unforgiving people isolate themselves and lose their connection with others.[23]

People who choose pardon and forgiveness, on the other hand, have healthier relationships, improved mental health, fewer symptoms of depression, and higher self-esteem. Their levels of stress and anxiety are reduced. They don't struggle with sudden angry outbursts or wrongly targeted hostility. They have lower blood pressure, a stronger immune system, and improved heart health.[24] With these physical and emotional benefits, why would any of us choose to be unforgiving?

The answer is simple: The human heart is fickle and duplicitous. Being fashioned into the Lord and Divine Master's instrument of peace means going against and moving beyond the ego's centripetal self-centeredness and selfishness. It requires training the soul in the art and heart of forgiveness.

As an art, forgiveness is a learned process that is fraught with complexity. Though it can be taught with suggested exercises, each of us comes to it in our own way, in our own time. It is rarely instantaneous. Like lifting heavy weights, it is slowly acquired and needs to be practiced time and again. Even after a pardon has been offered, the temptation to revert back to serving the servant by holding on to a grudge and fueling resentment can remain.

The heart of this process is a radical self-denial like the kenotic selflessness I mentioned in chapter 2. We clear an interior space and renounce our attachment to an offense, the anger it engendered, and the desire for revenge and justice that arises. We are brutally honest with ourselves as we take a long, hard look at our sense of entitlement and its myriad effects on our relationships. Consequently, the process of forgiveness can be a struggle as we journey down its long and convoluted road.

The Witness of Esau

The Old Testament account of the fraternal twins Esau and Jacob is an ancient story of a perennial theme: sibling rivalry. The rivalry is foreshadowed in two details: the two struggled in the womb of their mother, Rebekah (Genesis 25:22); the younger Jacob came out of the womb gripping his older brother's heel as if trying to prevent Esau from becoming the firstborn (v. 26). Their relationship was complicated by parental favoritism: their father, Isaac, was biased toward Esau while their mother preferred Jacob (v. 28). The brothers were also opposites in temperament and ability: Esau was an impetuous nomadic hunter who sold his birthright to Jacob for a meal (vv. 29–34); Jacob was a cunning sedentary shepherd who, following his mother's scheme, wrested his elderly and near-blind father's blessing from the elder son (27:1–40). Pawns in their parents' rivalry with each other, Esau and Jacob contended in a relationship marred by competition, intrigue, deception, and hatred that culminated in Esau's desire to kill his younger brother (27:41).

The twins were separated for twenty years. One would presume Esau spent those years seething over the entitlement stolen from him by Jacob. When they finally met again, Jacob, "bowing himself to the ground seven times" (Genesis 33:3), was formal and laden with guilt as he referred to himself as "your servant" (v. 5) and called Esau "my lord" (v. 8). Even before Jacob spoke, the text reads, "But Esau ran to meet him, and embraced him, and fell on his neck and kissed him, and they wept" (v. 4). During the two decades of separation, Esau had traveled the road of mercy and come to a place of pardon and forgiveness.

I thought of the story of Esau and Jacob as I sat in a spiritual direction session with Janet.

"My brother is two years older than me and we are like oil and water," she said. "The family always gets together for the holidays and my husband and I never attend. It's just too difficult for me. When we did attend the holiday meals in the past, I would always leave angry and hurt over Troy's treatment of me. So we stopped going seven years ago. Now my mother is gravely ill, and I suspect this will be her last Christmas. I feel some internal pressure to join the family for the Christmas dinner. But I just don't know what to do about my feelings for Troy. I really don't want to cause a scene."

I reminded Janet about the story of Esau and Jacob. I told her that at their reunion, Esau had every reason to be angry and bitter at his younger brother. Jacob's timid deference suggested as much.

"And yet, granted it took twenty years, in the end, Esau found it in his heart to forgive his brother," I concluded.

"How did he get there? What did he have to do to let go of the hurt and offer forgiveness?" Janet asked.

I blushed and glanced out the window.

"I don't know. The Bible doesn't tell us."

'SEVENTY-SEVEN TIMES'

Jesus's teachings and example validate the Peace Prayer's petition to bring pardon where there is injury. Though the Gospel of Luke suggests repeated forgiveness whenever anyone says "I repent" (see Luke 17:3–4), implying contrition and an apology, the Gospel of Matthew renders Jesus's meaning in a very different way: When Peter asked if "seven times," the perfect number seven suggesting perfect forgiveness, was generous enough, Jesus suggests the limitless measure of "seventy-seven times" (see Matthew 18:21–22). He buttresses this statement with the parable of the unforgiving servant who is tortured until he paid off his entire debt (vv. 23–35). The parable concludes with the stark declaration, "So my heavenly Father will also do to every one of you, if you do not forgive your brother or sister from your heart" (v. 35). Three points are noteworthy about Matthew's interpretation.

First, in reply to Peter, there is no mention of contrition or regret. Like Esau's, forgiveness is never dependent on an apology. Jesus instinctively knew that some people never learn the social grace of offering an apology; for others, it is emotionally too challenging, exhausting, and expensive.

Demanding an apology betrays an insensitive arrogance that can be revealed in one's body language. The silent treatment, the cold shoulder, and arms crossed over the chest are nonverbal forms of communication that speak volumes about our lack of forgiveness.

Francis of Assisi might have been aware of how a sense of entitlement can be exposed by body language as insignificant as one's eyes. The saint gave this advice to a minister who was struggling with a sinful friar:

I should like you to prove that you love God and me, his servant and yours, in the following way. There should be no friar in the whole world who has fallen into sin, no matter how far he has fallen, who will ever fail to find your forgiveness for the asking, if he will only look into your eyes. And if he does not ask forgiveness, you should ask him if he wants it. And should he appear before you again a thousand times, you should love him more than you love me, so that you may draw him to God; you should always have pity on such friars.[25]

The eyes are the lamp of the soul (see Matthew 6:22), and they should proclaim an unconditional Christian pardon that frees the adversary from any prerequisites or requirements demanded by the injured person.

However, Jesus does not exonerate us from offering an apology when we ourselves are the adversary who inflicts the injury. He makes it the basis of worship: "So when you are offering your gift at the altar, if you remember that your brother or sister has something against you, leave your gift there before the altar and go; first be reconciled to your brother or sister, and then come and offer your gift" (Matthew 5:23–24). Mercy always comes before sacrifice (see Matthew 9:13; 12:7; Hosea 6:6).

Second, forgiveness is not whitewashing, glossing over, or repressing our feelings and emotions. It goes far beyond a superficial, polite "Oh, it was nothing" often said as we deposit a hurt in the heart. It does not condone the injury inflicted nor does it distort the gravity of the wrong done. It is an experience of the gratuity of grace that transforms our feelings and emotions—or, to use Jesus's expression, it must come "from the heart" (Matthew 18:35).

Third, the Lord and Divine Master reiterates the incentive to forgive our neighbor by predicating divine forgiveness on it. In the words of the Peace Prayer, "It is in pardoning that we are pardoned." Being two sides of the same coin, the forgiveness of God cannot be received unless the forgiveness of one's neighbor is given. Both the Lord's Prayer and the Sermon on the Mount remind us of this inherent connection (see Matthew 6:12, 14–15) as does the Letter to the Colossians: "Bear with one another and, if anyone has a complaint against another, forgive each other; just as the Lord has forgiven you, so you also must forgive" (3:13). Unfortunately, we are told to forgive with neither a path to pardon being indicated nor a method of forgiveness being taught.

THE PARABLE OF THE PRODIGAL SON

Like the story of Esau and Jacob, the parable of the prodigal son (Luke 15:11–32) is steeped in sibling rivalry—but in this case it is implicit, seething in the heart of the older son. We again see how a sense of entitlement can cause injury as the younger son demands the share of the property that would belong to him at his father's death. We don't hear about the father's emotional reaction to such a request. We just see his straightforward response: "So he divided the property between them" (v. 12).

The younger son left for a distant land and "squandered his property in dissolute living" (v. 13). His impetuousness and self-alienation are symbolized in his life among pigs and his hunger. His sense of entitlement injured his relationship both with his father and with himself. Like the guilt-ridden Jacob, the younger son, knowing that his status as son had been permanently lost, started the journey back home.

Did Jesus have Esau in mind when he spoke of the father's response on seeing his son on the road? "But while he was still far off, his father saw him and was filled with compassion; he ran and put his arms around him [literally 'falling upon the boy's neck,' the exact same response of Esau when we saw Jacob] and kissed him" (v. 20). The father interrupted the younger son's apology and instantly clothed him with robe, ring, and sandals. And then he called for a feast to celebrate.

Hearing the music, the dancing, and the news of his younger brother's return, the older brother remained outside, as years of seething anger rose to the surface. As he did with his younger son, the father ran out to his elder only to encounter that son's sense of entitlement: "Listen! For all these years I have been working like a slave for you, and I have never disobeyed your command; yet you have never given me even a young goat so that I might celebrate with my friends" (v. 29). His imagination ran wild as he exaggerated his younger brother's sin with the claim that he "devoured your property with prostitutes" (v. 30).

We again don't know the father's emotional response to the older son's sense of entitlement and stubbornness. He tried to reassure the eldest of his position of privilege. And then we hear the justification "to celebrate and rejoice" (v. 32) coming from a fatherly heart overflowing with pardon and forgiveness for both sons.

Did the older son find the path to pardon and enter the celebration? The parable does not say.

The ABCs and D of Forgiveness

In parables and prayer, Jesus clearly spoke about the need to pardon. Some ancient Lukan manuscripts have him setting the example himself as he hung from the cross and prayed for his persecutors, "Father, forgive them; for they do not know what they are doing" (Luke 23:34). Though the injunction and example to pardon are clear, a method to train the soul in the art and heart of forgiveness is sorely lacking in Scripture. Being reminded of the necessity to forgive without being shown how to do it is like telling someone, "You must lose weight," and then refusing to teach the person a method of dieting or exercising. That easily leads to confusion, guilt, and alienation.

Have you ever wanted to forgive and move on from an injury but just didn't know how to do it? That dilemma can be so frustrating, demoralizing, and discouraging.

To walk in the footsteps of the Lord and Divine Master and sow the seeds of pardon require a practical method that leads us down the footpath of forgiveness. Here's one that I call the "ABCs and D of Forgiveness."

A: Acknowledge the injury and the feelings that arise.
Painful emotions need to be respected and validated before they can be released.

Some people hesitate to accept a feeling that they perceive as inappropriate, uncomfortable, negative, or unhealthy. They shy away from anger or emotional hurt. Or they feel the need to apologize for feeling how they feel. But a feeling is just that—a feeling. It's neither positive nor negative, right nor wrong—it's neutral. Its moral character is not determined by its nature but by its expression. We only can begin to put a feeling to rest by first recognizing and validating it. That happens by accepting and feeling the feeling. Extroverts especially find it helpful to share the injury and the feeling with someone. Friendship provides a vital ministry in this regard.

Some men are like Dennis. He has difficulty admitting his feelings and emotions around inflicted hurts and wounds. He considers the feelings that arise from hurts to be a sign of weakness. He prefers to shrug them off, forcing the emotions to go underground. His anger and resentment toward others often come out after he has downed a few beers.

When an emotion is swept under the carpet, it often finds expression—emotions by their very nature must be emoted—in unhealthy behaviors centered on food, drink, drugs, gambling, or sex. Acknowledging and accepting a feeling arising from an injury in a wholesome way is the first step toward forgiveness.

B: Where is the blockage?

Even after eight years, Darlene continues to withhold forgiveness because her sense of entitlement demands an apology from Richard. She seems oblivious to the fact that this demand is a blockage to forgiveness; it keeps her bound to her ex-husband and gives him continued power over her. Forgiveness would free her from both the emotional rope that still binds her to Richard and the control he continues to exercise over her.

When we feel blocked and unable to sow the seed of forgiveness, there are two good questions we can ask ourselves: What am I gaining by keeping this grudge alive and hanging on to its anger? What need is it satisfying inside of me? The answers will reveal the blockage—and heighten the awareness of the emotional energy it takes to keep stoking the fires of fury.

Sometimes we cannot forgive because we "need" an emotional payback or kickback. Anger and resentment satisfy our tit-for-tat, an-eye-for-an-eye sense of justice. Maybe our retained grudge indulges our sense of entitlement. "I deserve to be treated better," says the older son of the prodigal parable; true as that might be, that attitude doesn't help our blood pressure. Even though it is emotionally exhausting, we fuel the anger because it satisfies our taste for revenge and desire to see the adversary punished. Forgiveness requires the renunciation of the right for revenge.

Blockages can be based on the wrong idea of what pardon really is. Billy refuses to forgive because he mistakenly equates forgiveness with condoning the action or excusing the offense: "I am not going to give anyone a free pass to deliberately hurt me or permission to make me a doormat for injustice." Mary Anne's comment betrays her own misconception: "Forgiveness is living in denial. It is turning a deaf ear or blind eye to something that needs to be confronted." For years I refused to forgive my father because I mistakenly equated forgiveness with forgetting—and I can never forget the pain his decision to die has left upon my heart. Such misunderstandings can pose obstacles on the path to pardon.

Sometimes blockages to forgiveness are based upon cold, rational logic. "He should have known better!" or "What was she thinking?" can give us justification for withholding forgiveness. Exposing and exploring our thinking in prayer, conversation, or spiritual direction can sometimes break through the blockages and turn the *desire* to see punishment into the *decision* to offer pardon.

C: *Cauterize the residual resentment.*

Once we have exposed our misunderstandings and broken through our rational blockages, it is quite common to experience continued emotional pain over an injury. Consequently, we need to be proactive about deadening any lingering feelings or reactions.

These residual feelings can be purged through ritual, meditation, and prayer. I found it helpful to go to the cemetery and read a letter I had written to my father fifteen years after his death. I left the letter at his grave. That helped me to let go of my anger and hurt.

Some people find meditation helpful. They use a simple technique of breathing out the anger and breathing in peace and pardon. This practice of soul training brings them to a place of mercy and forgiveness.

One of my spiritual directees prefers the prayer of lament, expressing to God her anger and hurt while at the same time asking God to set her heart free from resentment and rage.

In each case, the fact of the injury remains, but one's feelings about it are gradually transformed or released.

I was taught another way to get rid of the residual resentment—in the confessional.

I was livid and my heart was pulverized with bitterness and rage over a betrayal by a friar who had been a dear friend of mine. Whenever I heard his name mentioned, I had the need to say cruel things about him and malign his reputation. I didn't hesitate to publicize his betrayal to others.

While on my annual retreat, I went to confession to a Trappist monk. I was tired of being angry and bitter but just didn't know how to move beyond the emotions. After confessing my anger and the sin of detraction, the monk just stared at me and took a deep breath.

"Albert," he said, "our abbot always reminds us of a wonderful spiritual practice when we are hurt by one of our brother monks. He tells us to pray daily for the well-being of the '*enemy*.'" He chuckled as he emphasized that word and continued, "'Even if you don't mean it,' the abbot says, 'you have to start somewhere.' I have found it to be a helpful exercise. I've noticed how, after a few days or weeks of praying for a monk who injured me, my anger dissipates and I'm back to my old self. So this is what I'm giving you for a penance: I want you to pray for that friar's well-being. And not just today but every day, until you come to a place of forgiveness and your bitterness fades away."

I wasn't happy with the penance. I was tempted to question its appropriateness since I have always wondered if a priest could validly give you a lifelong penance, which I thought this would be. I still remember how, months later, I would squirm in prayer as I prayed for Mark's well-being.

But a penance is a penance, and I kept praying for the friar. Daily. On a Thursday morning in March 2019, as I always do toward the end of my prayer time, I turned my attention to the list of people for whom I had promised to pray. Three years later, Mark's name was still on the list. But something was different this morning. As I prayed for his well-being, I felt a surge of desire that he be happy. The anger had evaporated. The rancor had disappeared. I happened upon pardon and forgiveness.

The challenge of Jesus, "But I say to you, Love your enemies and pray for those who persecute you" (Matthew 5:44), is wise and tested advice. Praying for an adversary opens the heart to the gratuity of grace. Over days, weeks, or in my case years, we find the bitterness and hurt dislodging until they finally recede from view.

Sometimes ridding ourselves of residual resentment can be aided by putting ourselves in the offender's shoes. Was the person really motivated by a deliberate, malicious intent? Were circumstances beyond the person's control the real cause of the inflicted injury? What emotional or physical pain motivated the offender to react or treat us in the way we were treated? As we grow in the understanding of the adversary's predicament or circumstances, compassion leads us to catharsis.

D. Decide to move on.

Forgiveness is not a feeling. It is a decision, an act of the will, a resolution, a firm choice to free ourselves from the continued influence and control of the adversary. While the ABCs of forgiveness are focused on the centripetal force of the self, the D of decision activates the centrifugal force of the Spirit as we move beyond the past. As we deliberately and intentionally walk the footpath beyond the ego's injury, we find ourselves being blessed with spiritual maturity: Wounds are often the womb of wisdom.

Because forgiveness is a process and our hearts are finicky, we might be tempted to revisit the scene of the crime and throw another log on the fires of fury. When that occurs, we remind ourselves that we have made the rational decision to pardon and get on with life. We recommit to the decision. With every recommitment to forgiveness, we take another step forward in the footsteps of the Lord and Divine Master and becoming his instrument.

A Note on Reconciliation

Called Chiesa Nuova ("New Church")—the last church built in Assisi in 1615—the late Renaissance style church was built over the home of Pietro Bernardone, the father of Saint Francis. The high altar is built over what is believed to have been the future saint's bedroom, and visitors can still visit both the shop where Pietro and Francis sold their cloth and the stairwell Pietro used to imprison his son for renouncing the family business.

In the small piazza outside Chiesa Nuova stands a bronze statue of the saint's parents designed and cast by Roberto Joppolo in 1984. There is an irony to the statue. Holding hands, mother and father have somber facial expressions as they look off in different directions, no doubt symbolic of the sadness between them: she faces forward, he to the right. They hold symbols of what separated Pietro from his son: Francis's mother, Lady Pica, holds the chains her husband used when he placed their son under house arrest and from which she released him; Pietro holds cloth, symbolic of the family business that his son had renounced.

Joppolo's bronze statue is an unfortunate testimony to an important reality. Though it takes only one person to pardon, it takes both people to reconcile. Because some injuries are indelible, forgiveness does not always lead to reconciliation and the healing of a relationship. Though we can hope that father, mother, and son finally walked the footpath to forgiveness, we have no evidence that they ever reconciled before their deaths. It's a sad paradox that our pardon and forgiveness sometimes are aching reminders of lost treasures.

We pray to be instruments of peace in the Peace Prayer. That transformation occurs as we serve the Lord and Divine Master and train our souls in the ABCs and D of forgiveness. When we commit and recommit to the process of sowing pardon amid an injury, we witness to the gratuity of grace that moves us from selfishness to selflessness.

....

CUSTOMIZE YOUR TRAINING

- What has helped you pardon and forgive an adversary? When has it led to reconciliation with the person who injured you? What do you do when an adversary refuses to reconcile with you?
- What emotional, mental, and logical blockages continue to impede you from pardoning an adversary? What strategies can you use to overcome them?

....

SPIRITUAL COOLDOWN

Ponder

Put away from you all bitterness and wrath and anger and wrangling and slander, together with all malice, and be kind to one another, tenderhearted, forgiving one another, as God in Christ has forgiven you. (Ephesians 4:31–32)

Imitate

As we have said before, the brothers suffered many things both from grown-up people and from children, and sometimes even their wretched garments were filched from them. When this happened, the servants of God remained naked, since, in accordance with the Gospel, they wore only a tunic; they did not even claim the return of the stolen garments; only if someone, moved by pity, chose to give them back, the brothers accepted them gladly. Sometimes they were pelted with mud; sometimes jesters put dice into their hands inviting them to play; others pulled at them from behind, dragging them along by their cowls. These and other similar pranks were played on them by people who considered them of no account and tormented them as they pleased. The brothers suffered all this, hunger, thirst, cold, nakedness, and many immense tribulations, firmly and patiently, as Saint Francis had bidden them. They were not dejected, they never cursed their tormentors; but like men whose faces are set to a great reward they exulted in tribulations and joyfully prayed to God for their presecutors. (*Legend of the Three Companions*, 40)

Pray
Lord and Divine Master, may the grace of your forgiveness touch my heart and prod me to share pardon and forgiveness with anyone who injures me. Amen.

....

CHAPTER FIVE

Where There Is Doubt, Faith

Joseph doesn't recall as a child being affirmed or encouraged to use his gifts and talents. He has no memory of his parents telling him he was lovable.

"What I remember most about my childhood," he told me, "was that my parents always compared me to my brother, Dan, and reminded me that neither my academic nor athletic ability was as good as his. He was the star of the family, and I spent my early years in his shadow. I also remember having lots of fears. Like many kids, I had a fear of the dark—but mine stuck around until I was in the third or fourth grade. I also had a fear that my parents would abandon me because they were just so unhappy with me. I had virtually no self-esteem in high school. My classmates teased and bullied me, and, frankly, I was okay with that because it made me realize that at least they noticed me and took an interest in me, though that kind of negative attention wasn't what I really wanted or needed. I don't remember exactly when it was, but somewhere along the line I told myself, 'I'll show them. One day they will all come to respect me.'"

As he reminisced during this spiritual direction session, I started to understand why Joseph was sometimes abusive toward his coworkers. It became clear why he had become such an over-achiever who was controlling, demanding, and manipulative.

Without being aware of it, he was seeking, demanding, and grabbing from others what he never was given in his childhood. He was looking outside for personality props such as power, control, and success to fill up his childhood deficiency.

THE CHALLENGE OF PARENTING

Parents have one of the toughest jobs on earth. Their challenge is to instill faith and self-confidence in their children. They must treat each child as if he or she was the only child. They must fight the temptation to compare siblings, lest one child feels unaccepted or inadequate, like Joseph. Parents need to encourage with enthusiasm while affirming with affection. In the words of the Peace Prayer, they should sow faith in a field prone to the weeds of self-doubts and fears.

How do parents train the souls of their children in confidence, self-esteem, and faith in themselves? Some practical ways include:

- *Give a child choices.* Parents can grow a child's sense of empowerment by preselecting two or three options from which a child can choose. This could range from what snacks to eat to what toys to buy.
- *Be patient and allow a child to do certain tasks at one's own speed.* This builds confidence. Intervening for the sake of expediency—"Mommy can do it faster than you"—can be counterproductive and discouraging for a child.
- *Teach a child that making mistakes is a part of life.* No one is perfect. Trying to instill perfectionism in a child will only lead to frustration and low self-esteem. Parents are challenged to love as unconditionally as possible.
- *Don't compare siblings.* This leads to a spirit of competition in which one child emerges the victim. Each child is individual and unique.

- *Never belittle a child.* Each child has a personal pace in growing up. Some are fast learners while others are more conventional. Children also differ in learning styles.
- *Let a child be a child.* Children are not meant to be little adults. If you attempt to put an adult's head on a child's body, you'll end up creating a monster.
- *Give a child chores.* This helps to build competence and instills responsibility and pride in contributing to family life.
- *Offer a child appropriate praise.* Exaggerated praise can backfire by lowering the bar of acceptable behavior. Self-confidence arises as a child tries, fails, and tries again.
- *Play with your child.* One-on-one time gives a child the feeling of being noticed.

Children who have been blessed and raised with healthy self-esteem and faith in themselves grow up with a realistic sense of who they are. As adults, they set appropriate boundaries and are poised and confident in what they say and do. They have a spirit of adventure and never fear embracing and celebrating the new and unknown. Because no one threatens them, they don't hesitate to acknowledge and compliment others' talents and accomplishments.

If parents are inattentive or insensitive to the individual needs of each child, they risk raising children who become adults with behaviors symptomatic of self-doubts. Bryan doesn't hesitate to use humor to make snide remarks to his family and friends. Kathy is sarcastic, always highlighting the difference she perceives in what someone says and does. Eric is a bully who has a habit of using harsh words and aggressive behaviors to get colleagues to comply to his demands. Peter's cries for attention, affirmation, and affection lead him to buy drinks in bars for people who are clearly not interested in his company. Michael constantly reminds you of the famous and powerful people he calls friends. Donna is obsessed with knowing everyone's business. Dan posts on Facebook a picture of himself with an award, commenting "I just was named Employee of the Year" and then tweets, "You want your company to hire me! I'm the best of over 800 employees!!!" Doubts entice desperate people to do desperate things.

EXAMPLES FROM SCRIPTURE

King Herod was a stunted, desperate adult who had doubts about himself. He was deeply agitated by the birth of a newborn baby announced by the wise men from the east. Learning of the approximate time of the birth, he slaughtered all boys two years old or younger in and around the village of Bethlehem. He clearly wanted to wipe out any future competition that could potentially threaten his authority and control of the people. His use of brute power as a personality prop to alleviate any self-doubts and competition from others was as tragic as the deaths of the Holy Innocents (see Matthew 2:1–18).

John's Gospel records the Lord and Divine Master meeting a stunted adult desperate for affirmation and affection. While passing through Samaria, Jesus encountered a woman at Jacob's well (see John 4:1–42). Because he had no bucket, he asked the woman for a drink. The request immediately developed into talking about the soulful thirst that everyone experiences. The conversation occurs on two separate levels as the woman talked about the topic literally while Jesus addressed the deeper thirst for wholeness and happiness that is part of the human condition. Leading the woman to his deeper level, Jesus asked her about her husband. When the Samaritan woman said she did not have one, Jesus reminded her of her past five husbands and "the one you have now is not your husband" (v. 18).

The point raises questions for the attentive reader: Assuming Samaritan Jewish law was similar to traditional Jewish practice, how did the woman end up with five husbands, two more than allowed by traditional Judaism? Did the woman's self-doubts keep the centripetal force operative in her adult life as she sought and grabbed in relationships what she was never trained to discover in herself as a child? When she didn't get what she wanted or became bored with a relationship, did she end it and go on to another? We can only pause, ponder, and postulate. Jesus's stark statement about her present relationship, however, is a reminder that love is a centrifugal force that selflessly catapults us to a firm, deliberate, lifelong commitment to another.

SOWING FAITH IN STUNTED ADULTS

A few years ago, I was privileged to be a speaker at a three-day, national Catholic men's conference. One morning, over snacks in the Speakers' Lounge, I had the good fortune of meeting someone whose writings have had a profound impact on me. After introductions and small talk, I asked him, "So what have you been up to lately?"

"Two months ago, I was in Sydney and Perth giving some lectures. After this conference, I'm off to London to lead a retreat. After that retreat, I go to Toronto and then Calgary. In the midst of all of that, I have to finish a manuscript due to my publisher at the end of May. I'm just so busy, you know. I rarely have time to breathe and be myself."

Scanning the room and seeing someone he knew, he condescendingly tapped me on the arm and said, "Well, I must away, as they say. It was nice meeting you." As he walked away, he turned his head to the right and asked the wall, "And where does your next gig take you?"

"Peoria," I mumbled as I watched him approach and interrupt two people, exclaiming, "Oh, Jim, it's so nice to see you again!"

It can sometimes be an eye-opener and real disappointment to meet someone who is famous or whom we admire. It's easy to forget that some creative, talented, and famous people are just like us: broken, needy, riddled with self-doubts. They have clay feet and their own personal issues and their own personal coping skills. Like us, some might live each day cowering like a punished puppy or barking their way through the week with endless demands. Because of an inflated sense of entitlement, others might thrust themselves on people, becoming aggressive, difficult, and cruel. Some of these adults become paranoid, obsessively looking over their shoulders, constantly comparing themselves to others, and frequently feeling threatened. Still others become needy, desperately seeking attention, affirmation, and affection from anyone who shows the least bit interest in them. Or they might lean on their accomplishments and accolades to prop themselves up publicly. Attachments, pride, fame, a sense of entitlement, a busy schedule—and substance abuse, as happens with some Hollywood stars—sometimes medicate and alleviate the pain of self-doubts and feelings of inadequacy. I wonder if that speaker I met purposely overbooked his schedule to guarantee he couldn't "breathe and be myself." Maybe he feared meeting the empty person he might encounter.

The Letter to the Ephesians states, "Let no evil talk come out of your mouths, but only what is useful for building up, as there is need, so that your words may give grace to those who hear" (Ephesians 4:29). Soul training is steeped in the gratuity of grace, and sometimes we are called to be the instruments of that very grace by building up those weakened by doubts. How do we do that?

As Ephesians suggests, with our words of encouragement. We acknowledge the person's skills, encourage their talents, and affirm their goodness. We let them feel noticed. Words take on a life of their own and can have an impact, sometimes long after we have spoken them.

More important than our words, though, is our presence—and our attentive silence. As spiritual directors and counselors know, a loving presence is a tender power that can pull back the curtain to reveal a desperate adult child who is orchestrating the terrors of the Wizard of Oz. The Lord and Divine Master modeled this very presence when he encountered the Gerasene demoniac (see Mark 5:1–17; Luke 8:26–37), the woman caught in adultery (see John 8:1–11), the sinner who wept at his feet (see Matthew 26:6–13; Mark 14:3–9; Luke 7:36–50), and the rich young man (see Matthew 19:16–30; Mark 10:17–31; Luke 18:18–30). Being an instrument of God who plants the seeds of faith and confidence in the field of doubts can be as simple as putting an arm around someone's shoulder or lending a listening ear.

THE DESCENT OF DOUBTS

Doubts can arise not only in relationship to our parents and our upbringing but also in relationship to God and our soul training.

A committed Catholic, Terry decided two years ago to commit to thirty minutes of daily prayer. Amid shuttling her three children back and forth to school and extracurricular activities, cooking dinner for her family, and doing the daily housework, she has managed to find the time to be faithful to her decision. Her daily prayer has been a source of tremendous consolation, a time for heightening her awareness of God's presence in her life, and an excellent preparation for her attendance at the Sunday liturgy.

About six months ago, however, her prayer became very dissatisfying and a real struggle. It no longer gave her the lighthearted feelings of peace and consolation it had given in the past. Her prayer was hard, distracted, and "sometimes dull as dirt. I must be doing something wrong. I feel lost. Did I take the wrong turn somewhere?" she asked me.

She began wondering if there really and truly is a God. Her prayer backfired as she began to think she had wasted two years simply having a monologue with herself when she thought she was in dialogue with God. These doubts scared her. "Two years ago, I would never have allowed myself to even entertain such thoughts," she stated emphatically.

The Sunday Eucharist no longer charged her spiritual batteries. Instead, it became a real challenge and drain just to show up. "It's virtually impossible to remain attentive as I find myself thinking about everything except what is occurring during Mass," she admitted with embarrassment.

"I feel discouraged and defeated and a failure. After two years of prayer, I have nothing to show for them—and I mean that literally. I have no faith, no hope." She sighed as her eyes glistened with tears.

Doubts, Disappointments, and Disasters
Terry is mired in the desert of doubts. It's a harsh reality. A painful experience. A devastating source of confusion that makes her feel abandoned and forgotten.

Doubts strip us of faith's padding that helps us endure the rough and tough times. They rob us of the spiritual nourishment that once gave us so much comfort and stamina and motivation. They dampen our spiritual fervor, inspiration, and spiritual fire. Doubts discourage, deter, and dissuade soul training.

Doubts make us feel deflated and vulnerable as the deficiencies of our faith are exposed. Questions about God's love, presence, and providence hinder our vision as we struggle to feel our way and stumble through the day. Pious thoughts and beliefs that once were beacons of light guiding us through the fog are now extinguished. Like Terry, we might even have misgivings and skepticism about God's very existence.

Our favorite spiritual practices, such as prayer, fasting, and almsgiving, that were like daily or weekly aerobic exercises for our soul training, suddenly become uninviting and distasteful. Even the sacraments, once sources of refreshment and encouragement, devolve into sources of tedium and distraction and exhaustion.

Doubts, uncertainty, and questions also arise when people or events challenge and confront our fears and the personality props of attachments, the need to be in control, and our sense of entitlement. We fear ill health and are suddenly diagnosed with cancer. We must bury a loved one. We lose our job. We are treated unfairly. "Why did this happen? What did I do to deserve this?" we ask.

As an architect, Bryce hoped one day to build his family dream home in California. That day came and, for six years, he and his family enjoyed a wonderful life and home in Sonoma County. But the Kincade Fire of 2019 left behind only their home's foundation. "It was more than just our home, Father," he told me in a phone call, "it was becoming a womb for memories and experiences. Why did God allow this to happen? Isn't he in charge?"

Disappointments and disasters give birth to spiritual doubts and crises similar to what Terry was experiencing. Jesus himself was not immune to them. "Greatly disturbed" at the sight of Mary and some Jews weeping over the death of Lazarus, Jesus himself wept (see John 11:33, 35). He struggled emotionally in the garden of Gethsemane as he sought to accept his impending death (see Matthew 26:36–46; Luke 22:39–46). And on the cross, he began to pray Psalm 22, "My God, my God, why have you forsaken me?", a plea for deliverance from suffering and hostility (see Matthew 27:46; Mark 15:34).

DOUBTS LEAD TO MATURE FAITH

People mistakenly believe that soul training is just like a sports activity or physical exercise—the more you practice, the easier it becomes. This notion was the root of Terry's belief that she had become a spiritual failure after two years of prayer. But soul training has a logic all its own and is riddled with paradox. Consider some of Jesus's puzzling statements:

- "For those who want to save their life will lose it, and those who lose their life for my sake, and for the sake of the gospel, will save it" (Mark 8:35).
- "Whoever wants to be first must be last of all and servant of all" (Mark 9:35).
- "But it is not so among you; but whoever wishes to become great among you must be your servant, and whoever wishes to be first among you must be slave of all" (Mark 10:43–44).
- "Very truly, I tell you, unless a grain of wheat falls into the earth and dies, it remains just a single grain; but if it dies, it bears much fruit" (John 12:24).
- "Enter through the narrow gate; for the gate is wide and the road is easy that leads to destruction, and there are many who take it. For the gate is narrow and the road is hard that leads to life, and there are few who find it" (Matthew 7:13–14).
- "For many are called, but few are chosen" (Matthew 22:14).
- "Again I tell you, it is easier for a camel to go through the eye of a needle than for someone who is rich to enter the kingdom of God" (Matthew 19:24).
- "Do not think that I have come to bring peace to the earth; I have not come to bring peace, but a sword" (Matthew 10:34).

- "If you had faith the size of a mustard seed, you could say to this mulberry tree, 'Be uprooted and planted in the sea,' and it would obey you" (Luke 17:6).

Though we mistakenly think we are in control of our soul training as we pray, fast, and give alms, the reality is that soul training depends upon the gratuity of grace. And that grace has a dark side that can be disconcerting, disruptive, distressing, distasteful, and subversive. Its wild, unruly, and uncontrollable nature sometimes leads to the descent of doubts ("Does God really love me unconditionally?"), an apparent absence of divine action ("I feel like God has disappeared from my life"), an abyss of alienation ("I have nothing to show for all my years of believing"). Grace challenges our spiritual smugness, self-righteousness, and sense of entitlement. It comes into our lives and gradually erases every expression of our selfishness while it stretches us and remolds us into the "new self" (Colossians 3:10) that reflects the image of Christ. Painful as it is, the result is precious. As Paul so aptly exclaimed, "And it is no longer I who live, but it is Christ who lives in me. And the life I now live in the flesh I live by faith in the Son of God, who loved me and gave himself for me" (Galatians 2:20).

We need to remind those who have descended into doubts that this experience is a normal development initiated by grace. It naturally happens if we are faithful to soul training. Ironically, the more one serves the Lord and Divine Master, the harder soul training becomes. This is a painful reminder that soul training is not a matter of sheer willpower or human determination and resolve.

Remember Mother Teresa's image of being God's pencil? Like any other instrument being fashioned, a pencil needs to be sharpened. And not just once but time and again. Whether it's the first or fifteenth time, each requires a kenotic selflessness, a letting go, an activation of the Spirit's force. That movement from centripetal selfishness to centrifugal selflessness, of its very nature, requires sharpening one's blunt thoughts about God and a radical rethinking of the nature of faith.

Consequently, when doubts descend, my faith is not disappearing; it is maturing. And so, during this process of spiritual maturation and sometimes painful belief-whittling, I remind myself that the spiritual path to God is paved with persistence. I continue to open myself to the gratuity of God's grace with my soul training. That is all I can do. This is not the time to take a break or change my routine as inclined as I might be to do just that.

"Sit with your doubts and questions," I told Terry, "not suppressing them or judging and condemning yourself. These very doubts and questions are watering the ground for a faith with roots far deeper than smug, pietistic, or adolescent beliefs. These doubts might continue for weeks, months, or a season of life. But sooner or later, your fidelity to soul training will lead to a trust-filled stance that, instead of making these doubts and questions disappear, will absorb them and use them as the foundation of mature faith."

Though it went against her natural inclination, Terry took my advice. She continued with her commitment to daily prayer. Most days it was distracted and even unsettling as she continued to sit with her doubts. But over a period of months, a glint of light suddenly began breaking through her doubts.

"It didn't make my feelings of failure and questions about God completely disappear. But it did give me encouragement to stick with my prayer commitment," she recently said. "And before I knew it, my suspicions and questions were riddled with shafts of light, transforming them into a dazzling, star-filled night resplendent in beauty. I still had my doubts but was able to reverence them while rediscovering my faith in God."

The paradox of soul training had become real for Terry. Responding to the gratutity of grace, she had her thoughts about God and the spiritual life upended. Grace had disrupted and challenged her beliefs only to transform them into mature faith.

The Peace Prayer challenges us to offer the shade of self-confidence and the refreshment of persistent, God-centered faith to those who walk in the desert of doubts occasioned by their upbringing or their soul training. In so doing, we fulfill our vocations as instruments of the Lord and Divine Master, instruments who remind a skeptical world of the gratuity of grace.

CUSTOMIZE YOUR TRAINING

- On a scale of one (low to nonexistent self-confidence) to four (filled with self-confidence and faith in oneself), how would you rate yourself? Reflect on your childhood and upbringing. Whom do you blame for your lack of self-esteem? Whom do you thank for instilling self-confidence? How was low or high self-esteem grown in you?

- Think back to the last time doubts about your faith descended on your soul. What feelings and emotions did the experience stir within you? How have you incorporated and absorbed those doubts and questions into your current understanding of God and the spiritual life?

SPIRITUAL COOLDOWN

Ponder
Truly I tell you, if you have faith and do not doubt, not only will you do what has been done to the fig tree, but even if you say to

this mountain, "Be lifted up and thrown into the sea," it will be done. (Matthew 21:21)

Imitate

For his safest haven was prayer; not prayer of a single moment, or idle or presumptuous prayer, but prayer of long duration, full of devotion, serene in humility. If he began late, he would scarcely finish before morning. Walking, sitting, eating, or drinking, he was always intent upon prayer. He would go alone to pray at night in churches abandoned and located in deserted places, where, under the protection of divine grace, he overcame many fears and many disturbances of mind. (Thomas of Celano, *The First Life of St. Francis*, 71)

Pray

Lord and Divine Master, through the gratuity of your grace, may my questions and doubts lead me to a deeper self-acceptance and more mature faith in you. Amen.

....

CHAPTER SIX

Where There Is Despair, Hope

Over the past four decades, I have sat and listened to many people who have been left behind by suicide. There was Marjorie who grieved the loss of her husband, Andrew. I still remember the sobs of Dexter who lost his teenage daughter about fifteen years ago. I remember Sharon, Troy, Jason, and Jennifer—total strangers yet, like me, sharing a special bond: we were left behind by the suicide of a parent, spouse, child, or friend.

My most recent encounter was with William and Dorothy. In their mid-forties, they were struggling not only to make sense of their son's death but also to rid themselves of the guilt that such a tragic death often leaves behind.

"Brian had everything going for him with a beautiful wife and a two-year-old daughter," Dorothy said as William nodded. "He returned from Iraq three months ago, and we were all so grateful he got back alive. 'They're a family again,' William said."

"But almost immediately," William interrupted as his eyes teared up, "I sensed something was wrong. He had trouble sleeping. Nightmares woke him up and he'd be all sweaty and restless. He said he couldn't concentrate and had a hard time reconnecting with Julie and their child. My heart broke when he looked at me with glassy eyes one afternoon and mumbled, 'Dad, I've lost interest in life.'"

"I suspected he suffered from PTSD," Dorothy continued, "and told him to make an appointment at the VA hospital."

"But we were too late. When Julie returned after picking Katie up from nursery school, she found Brian dead from a gunshot wound. We should have seen it coming—all the signs were there—and we didn't. I feel so terrible. I could have prevented this. I let him down as a father." William wiped his tears with his index finger.

Choking her words, Dorothy concluded, "He was such a good kid. And a good husband and father. And he insisted that they go to church every Sunday as a family. And now it's all wasted. I fear he's going to spend all eternity in hell for what he did and what we didn't do. Why did God let this happen?"

Every story of suicide is different. And yet the same in many ways. Each raises questions. Each is riddled with guilt. I've had more than fifty years to work through the questions and guilt raised by my father's death and have made my peace with them. Not everyone is as lucky.

Clear as the signs might be in hindsight, suicide is impossible to predict. It is always an unforeseen and unexpected tragedy.

I know that dying by one's own hand goes against our instinct to live, survive, and thrive. How could anyone in a right mind act against that instinct? Something must snap inside the victim.

I am convinced that God never judges a lifetime based upon a last, single act of desperation. How could he, if he is a God of love and justice? God doesn't judge with the quickness of a human heart.

And I am well aware that such a death is often shrouded in a mystery laden with burdens, illness, regrets, shame, struggles, or secrets. That mystery is rarely revealed to family and friends.

I slowly and gingerly shared my thoughts with William and

Dorothy. I was careful not to give them the impression that Brian's was simply "another suicide." It wasn't. Each life—and death—must be honored and reverenced as singular and unique. I quickly realized, though, that my thoughts about the human condition and God's wise, compassionate love were simply inadequate. Nothing I said could lift the veil of despair they felt over their son's death.

The Nature of Hope

Hope is not a feeling, sentiment, or affect. It is not a starry-eyed assurance, cheery conviction, or buoyant confidence. Nor is it passive optimism that, despite the situation, bullishly predicts, "It's all going to work out." It is beyond security and peacefulness.

Hope cannot be bought or taught. It can only be received and awakened. Saint Francis instinctively knew this when, seeking discernment before the San Damiano crucifix, he prayed, "And give me...certain hope..."[26]

The seed of hope is planted by God and celebrates the gratuity of grace. It is a gift, a blessing that strangely breaks ground and sprouts only during times of desperation, despair, despondency, and disaster—when the soul is parched.

To use another metaphor, it is like that sudden streak of light that comes out of nowhere and shoots across the midnight sky. Or a waxing crescent moon lighting up a forest clearing. Or the pulsating sheen of a faraway comet. It illumines.

Once given and awakened, hope adjusts our vision from the centripetal, focused on the self, to the centrifugal, focused on the power, providence, and protection of God. As the psalmist sings:

> For God alone my soul waits in silence,
> for my hope is from him.

He alone is my rock and my salvation,
 my fortress, I shall not be shaken.
On God rests my deliverance and my honor;
  my mighty rock, my refuge is in God. (Psalm 62:5–7)

Hope rivets the attention to the horizon and one can no longer
look back or go back to sleep. It is the stamina to stand in total
darkness before the dawn. It is an interior spark that propels
Karen, diagnosed with Hodgkin's lymphoma, to another day. It
was the ray of light that glowed in Derrick Hamilton, unjustly
locked in solitary confinement for twenty-three years by the state
of New York for a murder he did not commit. It is the anchor for
those feeling adrift in grief, bankruptcy, or exile. It sustains.

Peter writes of the birth and emergence of a vibrant hope—what
he calls a "living hope"—rooted in the reality of the resurrection: "Blessed be the God and Father of our Lord Jesus Christ!
By his great mercy he has given us a new birth into a living hope
through the resurrection of Jesus Christ from the dead" (1 Peter
1:3). This living hope, founded on the fidelity of God, transforms
every tomb into a womb of new life, every crisis into a potential
expression of divine creativity, every peril into another opportunity for the power of God to be revealed.

Though God's instruments pray to sow the seed of hope in those
who despair, they cannot. All they can do is till the field with the
desire that the forlorn and forsaken are receptive to hope's illumi-
nation and sustenance.

Spiritual Direction

Because living hope is a grace grounded in the power, providence,
and protection of God, there are five spiritual practices that can
train the soul to be receptive to it. These practices are helpful not
only for those who despair but also for the instruments of God
who till their field.

Shirley has been coming to me for spiritual direction for more than five years. Our fifty-minute sessions have covered a vast range of topics: her prayer life, the action of God's grace in her family life, the challenges of discerning what God might be asking of her, and the struggle to find meaning when life gets difficult.

Shirley occasionally suffers from anxiety that causes her undue confusion. When it rears its head, her anxiety is typically centered on what she perceives as her lack of total commitment to God. "I can give God more. I can do better," she tells me. She begins to worry that God is dissatisfied with her. She becomes restless. That makes her tired and irritable. And that brings on tense muscles, panic attacks, and irrational fears. It's a vicious cycle that strikes her about twice a year.

As her spiritual director, I can serve as Shirley's memory for the gratuity of grace in her life. Having witnessed her anxiety attacks several times, I know they are rooted in a less-than-satisfying image of God and the high octane spiritual expectations she has placed on herself. I speak of her spiritual progress that has become so apparent to me over the past five years. I remind her of the goodness and unconditional love of God: "Don't forget, as Jesus says in chapter five of the Gospel of Matthew, God lets the sun rise on the evil and on the good, and sends rain on the righteous and the unrighteous" (see Matthew 5:45). I let her know how encouraged I am by her impressive commitment to spiritual formation and the spiritual life. And I reiterate a basic spiritual principle: "This is God's work, not yours. Everything is a result of his grace and not your effort." Reminded again, Shirley relaxes as hope breaks through her fears and anxiety.

Spiritual direction as a practice of remembering and pondering the action of God in our lives is an excellent way to stay grounded in the gratuity of grace. This spiritual practice keeps the field of our souls watered and our hearts alert to the God of surprise and disguise. It promotes the stance of the farmer who sleeps and rises night and day, not knowing how the seed sprouts and grows (see Mark 4:26–29). It can open a person to living hope.

WORDS AND PRAYER

Two more practices that facilitate openness and receptivity to hope in ourselves and others are words of encouragement and the prayer of intercession. A supportive email, a kind word, a handwritten note, a bouquet of flowers, a pat on the back, a post on Facebook, all are practical reminders that one is not alone, that one can count on the support of family and friends. Words and actions of friendship, consolation, and encouragement offer an oasis and sense of community to those who isolate themselves as they bear the weight of disheartenment, desperation, and distress.

I met Sister Agnes twenty-five years ago. A Xaverian Missionary Sister of Mary, she had been a missionary in the West African country of Sierra Leone. She told me that she and six other Xaverian sisters had been taken hostage by rebels in 1995. Held captive for more than three months, the seven had no idea whether they would ever be released. As the weeks dragged on, the sisters became despondent as they thought everyone had forgotten them. One morning, allowed to listen to the *BBC World News*, they heard Pope John Paul II encouraging the world to continue praying for their release. Sister Agnes told me how that announcement reinvigorated all seven sisters in their daily trials as hostages.

Knowing that one is being prayed for can open a person's soul to be receptive to hope. More than strong-arming God to get what we want or doing a rain dance long enough to obtain the desired results, the prayer of intercession, like spiritual direction and words of encouragement, is a reminder that the gratuity of grace is never exhausted and never expires. This simple knowledge leaves behind a furrow in the field of the desperate and despairing.

COMPASSION

Michelle, a retired teacher, reminds us of a fourth spiritual practice for training the soul to be receptive to hope. In late 2018, while visiting her younger cousin who is a newspaper reporter in southern Texas, Michelle heard about Ursula, the colloquial name for the Central Processing Center, the largest immigration and detention center run by the Border Patrol and the Customs and Border Protection Agency. Opened in McAllen, Texas, in 2014, it is a 77,000-square-foot former warehouse that was leased and modified by the federal government to hold 1,000 children. Michelle's heart broke when she heard that the undocumented immigrant children were kept in large cages made of chain-link fencing.

Her sadness turned to anger when she read an ABC News report in June 2019. A medical doctor who was granted access to the facility said it felt worse than prison and described the conditions as tantamount to torture. The conditions included "extreme cold temperatures, lights on 24 hours a day, no adequate access to medical care, basic sanitation, water, or adequate food."[27]

Michelle felt compelled to do something. She asked around and heard about the hospitality ministry of Sister Norma Pimentel, the executive director of Catholic Charities of the Rio Grande Valley, at the Humanitarian Respite Center. Now, every month, Michelle makes the four-hour trip from San Antonio to McAllen to assist Sister Norma in whatever way she can for two to three days. Because she's a regular on the scene, some detainees refer to Sister Norma and Michelle as *Nuestra Esperanza* (Our Hope).

Compassion is a unique grace that will never destroy a person. It simply stretches the size of the heart and makes it more tender and loving. Compassionate people like Sister Norma and Michelle enter the darkness and suffering of others and become incarnations of living hope and strength. Their presence is potent since their care, concern, and actions help the despairing to endure—and sometimes provide just the right amount of moisture to help God's seed of hope to break ground in arid souls.

LOOKING TO THE SAINTS

We can open ourselves and others to the possibility of living hope by reading and remembering the stories of some of the great figures in Scripture and the spiritual tradition.

In chapter 4 of the Letter to the Romans, Paul recommends Abraham, the father of our faith, as a model of hope. Anchored in God's promise and hoping against hope, "[Abraham] believed that he would become 'the father of many nations,' according to what was said, 'So numerous shall your descendants be'" (v. 18). His old age ("for he was about a hundred years old") and his wife's barrenness did not cause his hope to flinch or waver (v. 19). Rather, because his hope was grounded in God, Abraham was "fully convinced that God was able to do what he had promised" (v. 21). In the very midst of the incredulity of his situation—old age and infertility—a living hope broke ground and blossomed.

Cleopas and another disciple were devastated by the death of Jesus. Their hope "that [Jesus] was the one to redeem Israel" (Luke 24:21) had been dashed. Their self-centered disappointment and despair blinded them to the identity of the stranger who walked with them to Emmaus (v. 16). As this stranger reminded them and explained the prophetic declarations that the Messiah had to suffer and die "and then enter into his glory" (v. 26), a flame of hope was lit in each of them as they said to each other in hindsight, "Were not our hearts burning within us while he was talking to us on the road, while he was opening the scriptures to us?" (v. 32) Disappointment and despair became the womb for promise, expectation, and hope.

The fourteenth century gave birth to a marvelous woman of hope. Julian of Norwich was an anchoress who lived a life of confined isolation, prayer, poverty, and chastity, in Norwich, England. She was known to give spiritual advice and counsel to those who came to her cell attached to the church in Norwich.

Hers were tumultuous times: The Black Death and its subsequent outbreaks killed at least half of the city's population. The Peasants' Revolt of 1381 brought the rebel forces of Geoffrey Litster into the town. The Lollards, who advocated for the reform of the Catholic Church, were being burned at the stake by order of Norwich's bishop.

In 1373 at the age of thirty, perhaps before she began her life as an anchoress, Julian became seriously ill. On May 8, as a priest held up a crucifix at the foot of her bed and gave her the last rites of the Catholic Church, she saw Christ's body on the crucifix begin to bleed. Over the next couple of hours, she had fifteen visions of Jesus followed by a sixteenth the following night. Five days later, she fully recovered from her illness and began writing about her sixteen "showings." Twenty to thirty years later, she wrote a theological explanation of her visions consisting of eighty-six chapters.

Despite the Black Death, the Peasants' Revolt of 1381, and the killings of the Lollards, Julian wrote reassuringly about God's benevolence and love. Although many despaired of God's presence and concern, Julian optimistically wrote, "God is nearer to us than our own soul…Jesus answered with these words, saying: 'All shall be well, and all shall be well, and all manner of thing shall be well'…This was said so tenderly, without blame of any kind toward me or anybody else."[28] Julian discovered and carried the light of a living hope shining through the darkness of her times.

THE EFFECTS OF HOPE

Though hope can only be received and awakened, we can train the soul for its reception through the practices of spiritual direction, words and actions of encouragement, the prayer of intercession, compassion, and remembering the lives of the saints. When hope is planted and awakened, our lives change. What are some of its effects?

Despair descends when we feel helpless and trapped in a dire situation. When hope breaks ground, we feel empowered. It propels us into tomorrow even though the situation remains the same. I think of those with life-threatening diseases who valiantly face the day.

Despair descends when meaning disappears and our lives become flat and directionless. When hope is awakened, we recalibrate our lives and rediscover meaning and purpose. Hope returns the sparkle to life. I think of those in broken relationships who remain open to friendship and love.

Despair descends when a loved one dies, leaving us feeling abandoned and forsaken. When hope is offered and received, we begin to celebrate the life of our beloved and grow in the awareness of one day being with the deceased again for all eternity. I think of those left behind by suicide who live with peace of mind.

Hope empowers, enlightens, gives confidence and a sure footing, and blesses us with meaning and purpose. No wonder Paul considers it to be one of the three abiding virtues (see 1 Corinthians 13:13).

Though the Peace Prayer has us praying to sow the seeds of hope among those who despair, we know that is humanly impossible. As instruments of God, all we can do is train our souls and the souls of others to be open and receptive as we till the soil and await another experience of the gratuity of grace.

CUSTOMIZE YOUR TRAINING

- Think back to a moment in your life when you were on the verge of despair or were blanketed by despondency. How was hope given and awakened in you? How long did it take to get back to a peaceful life?

- This chapter mentions five spiritual practices to train the soul to be receptive to hope: spiritual direction, words and actions of encouragement, the prayer of intercession, compassion, and remembering the lives of the saints. What are others that you have discovered and practiced? How do you till the ground in the souls of the hopeless and despairing?

SPIRITUAL COOLDOWN

Ponder

No testing has overtaken you that is not common to everyone. God is faithful, and he will not let you be tested beyond your strength, but with the testing he will also provide the way out so that you may be able to endure it. (1 Corinthians 10:13)

Imitate

There was a brother, a man of deep spiritual life and already very old in the Order, who was a close friend of blessed Francis. It so happened at one time that he was a prey for many days to most serious and cruel diabolical suggestions. And so he fell into the deepest despair. He suffered from them every day, and all the more so since he was ashamed to go and confess them each time. He mortified himself in an excessive way by fasting, vigils, tears, and the discipline. He had been tormented daily for a long time when, by a divine disposition, blessed Francis came to that place. One day when Francis was walking around the friary with a brother and with the one who was tormented in this way, the blessed Father withdrew himself a little from the first brother, approached the one who was tempted and said to him: "My dear brother, I wish and order that from this moment on you need not confess those suggestions and temptations of the Devil to anyone. Fear not: they have done no injury to your soul whatsoever. But every time you are troubled by these suggestions, I give you permission to recite the 'Our Father' seven times."

The brother rejoiced at these words and over the fact that he was not bound to confess these temptations, especially since he was ashamed to confess them every day, which aggravated his torment. He admired the holiness of his Father who had come to know of his temptations through the Holy Spirit. In fact, he had opened himself only to priests and he had changed priests often because he was ashamed to tell the extent of his weakness and his temptations to one priest alone. As soon as blessed Francis had spoken to him, he was freed of that great interior and external trial from which he had suffered so long. Through the grace of God and the merits of blessed Francis, he lived in great peace and tranquility of soul and body. (*The Legend of Perugia*, 7)

Pray
Lord and Divine Master, may my words and actions exude a holy confidence so that those who despair might be receptive to your gift of living hope. Amen.

CHAPTER SEVEN

Where There Is Darkness, Light

Light is a major and complex image in the Bible. At the very beginning of the biblical narrative, the first day of creation begins with God's command, "Let there be light" (Genesis 1:3).

Writing to the Corinthians, Paul links this first appearance of light in physical creation with the new creation that occurs in the life-changing moment of conversion: "For it is the God who said, 'Let light shine out of darkness,' who has shone in our hearts to give the light of the knowledge of the glory of God in the face of Jesus Christ" (2 Corinthians 4:6). Perhaps he was remembering his own experience on the road to Damascus when "suddenly a light from heaven flashed around him" (Acts 9:3). The biblical text concludes with a mention of light: "And there will be no more night; [God's servants] need no light of lamp or sun, for the Lord God will be their light" (Revelation 22:5).

Between the books of Genesis and Revelation, the imagery of light, both figuratively and literally, appears nearly two hundred times. It conquers darkness (John 1:5). It typically comes from outside the earthly realm and transforms it with splendor. A gift from above that permeates everyday life, light is a symbol of the transcendence and immanence of God (1 John 1:5; 1 Timothy 6:16).

It is a symbol for God's law, God's wisdom, and the word of God (Psalm 19:9; Wisdom 7:26; Psalm 119:105). It is God's garment (Psalm 104:2). It is reflected in the lives of those who encountered God, like Moses whose "skin of his face shone because he had been talking with God" (Exodus 34:29). Isaiah uses it to describe the Servant of Yahweh (42:6) and the charity offered to the oppressed, poor, homeless, naked, and afflicted (58:6–10). Light is associated with God and a godly life (Psalm 4:6; Proverbs 4:18; John 3:20).

In the letters written by or ascribed to Paul, light makes an appearance. Paul encourages the Romans, "Let us then lay aside the works of darkness and put on the armor of light" (Romans 13:12). The Letter to the Ephesians states, "For once you were darkness, but now in the Lord you are light. Live as children of light—for the fruit of the light is found in all that is good and right and true" (Ephesians 5:8–9). In the midst of "a crooked and perverse generation," the Philippians "shine like stars in the world" (Philippians 2:15).

Light is a central symbol in John's Gospel. The prologue describes the Word as the invincible, true light that took flesh among us and revealed "the glory as of the Father's only Son, full of grace and truth" (John 1:14). Jesus, "the light of the world," said those who follow in his footsteps would never walk in darkness but would have the "light of life" (John 8:12).

The Lord and Divine Master passed this light on to his followers and set their lives on fire. "You are the light of the world" (Matthew 5:14). Reminding them that a lamp is put on a lampstand and gives light to all in the house, he commissioned them: "In the same way, let your light shine before others, so that they may see your good works and give glory to your Father in heaven" (Matthew 5:16).

The community of believers continues to preserve and pass down this light from generation to generation. In the Rite of Christian Initiation of Adults, the newly baptized are reminded: "You have been enlightened by Christ. Walk always as children of the light and keep the flame of faith alive in your hearts."

GODLY LIGHT

Though legally blind and confined to a wheelchair for the past ten years, Theresa walks as a child of the light. At age seventy, her soul training in response to the gratuity of grace has consisted of reflecting on Scripture passages read to her and the slow and meditative repetition of the Jesus prayer. These practices have kept alive and fueled the flame of faith in her heart. They also help her to step squarely within the footsteps of the Lord and Divine Master and to walk "by faith, not by sight" (2 Corinthians 5:7).

Theresa's faith is a beacon for others. The medical assistants at the home where she resides have often confided their problems, concerns, and worries to her. Theresa compassionately listens and, from her luminous world of faith, freely shares the light of her wisdom. Grace has given her a clear-sighted vision.

SPIRITUAL VISION

The light of faith also gave another blind woman, Helen Keller, a clear-sighted vision. At nineteen months old, she lost her ability to see and speak after contracting scarlet fever or meningitis. When she was six years old, twenty-year-old Anne Sullivan, herself visually impaired with no reading or writing skills, was hired with the hope of teaching Helen Keller how to communicate. For the next forty-nine years, the blind would lead the blind as Sullivan's relationship with Keller evolved from instructor to governess to companion.

Helen Keller was once asked if there was anything worse than being blind. Her response is widely known. "The only thing worse than being blind is having sight but no vision."

Helen Keller's vision was rooted in her relationship with Jesus that broadened her outlook and expanded her influence. Among her friends were Alexander Graham Bell, Charlie Chaplin, and Mark Twain. She graduated as a member of Phi Beta Kappa from Radcliffe College of Harvard University, becoming the first deaf-blind person to earn a bachelor of arts degree. She campaigned for women's suffrage, labor rights, and opposed any and all military intervention even though her father had been a captain in the Confederate Army. She was a world-famous speaker, traveling to more than forty countries, and author of twelve books. She met every U.S. President from Grover Cleveland to Lyndon B. Johnson, the latter conferring on her the Presidential Medal of Freedom. The title of her revised and edited autobiography, *Light in My Darkness*, speaks volumes about the flame of her faith and the spiritual vision it gave her.

The Canticle of the Creatures

Almost eight hundred years before Theresa and Helen Keller, the flame of faith gave a third blind person another spiritual vision.

The last two years of Francis of Assisi's life are well documented in the written memories of Brothers Leo, Angelo, and Rufino, the small group of friars who cared for the saint in the final years of his life. According to their recollection, Francis spent more than fifty days at San Damiano, the small chapel where he experienced the call to rebuild the Church; it now had an adjacent convent housing Clare of Assisi and her community.

Francis was nearly blind. He suffered from trachoma, an eye disease characterized by frequent, abundant teary secretions and progressive corneal complications. The physical pain was so intense that he struggled to rest or sleep. Because he was unable to bear the light of the sun during the day or that of a fire at night, he lived in darkness. This physical infirmity was aggravated by other conditions resulting from his malnutrition.

The blind and frail saint lived in a small cell made of mats infested with mice. These mice so tormented Francis by climbing over him during his prayer, his meals, and as he struggled to sleep that both the saint and the companions considered them to be a demonic manifestation.

The early companions tell us that Francis went into a depression and started feeling sorry for himself. He prayed for patience in the face of his struggles.

God responded to Francis, "Well, brother, be glad and joyful in the midst of your infirmities and tribulations: as of now, live in peace as if you were already sharing my kingdom."[29]

This early promise of heaven was steeped in the gratuity of grace and helped Francis to accept his physical condition and circumstance. His darkened world suddenly became luminous with the divine presence as he saw creation in all its ordinariness and sacramentality. Though still sensitive to light, he began to compose one of the first songs ever written in the Umbrian dialect of Italy:

> All praise be yours, my Lord, through all that you have made,
>   And first my lord Brother Sun,
>   Who brings the day; and light you give to us through him.
>   How beautiful is he, how radiant in all his splendour!
>   Of you, Most High, he bears the likeness.[30]

The saint continued by recognizing his familial bonds with all creation and praised God in, by, and through Sister Moon, Sister Water, Brother Fire, and Sister Mother Earth.

He sang of the providence, generosity, and grace of God at every moment of life:

> All praise be yours, my Lord, through Brothers Wind and Air,
>> And fair and stormy, all the weather's moods,
>>> By which you cherish all that you have made.[31]

Hearing of the quarrel between the religious and civil authorities of Assisi, he later added how God is praised through instruments of peace and forgiveness:

> All praise be yours, my Lord, through those who grant pardon
>> For love of you; through those who endure
>> Sickness and trial.
>> Happy those who endure in peace,
>>> By you, Most High, they will be crowned.[32]

At the end of his life, he inserted a verse that praised Sister Death. He referred to her as "the second death,"[33] the first, no doubt, being when he renounced the centripetal pull of being a famous knight, emptied himself before Assisi's bishop and his father, and started following in the footsteps of the Lord and Divine Master.

In this tremendous moment of enlightenment, the frail saint was reminded of his early dream while still a knight when God asked if it was better to serve the servant or the Master:

> Praise and bless my Lord, and give him thanks,
>> And serve him with great humility.[34]

The Canticle of the Creatures is a testimony to Francis's soul training. Years of renouncing the personality props and clearing an interior space were rewarded with a sacramental vision of creation as a ladder that could lead one to God. Being God's instrument and sowing the seeds of love, forgiveness, and faith, led him to a mature vision that saw all creation bonded together in a familial relationship of grace. The secular had become sacred and the mundane mystical.

DEEDS OF LIGHT

Theresa, Helen Keller, and Francis of Assisi remind us that the interior fire of faith cannot be centered upon ourselves. Our faith is centrifugal and must radiate outward, giving light to others and brightening their lives (see Matthew 5:16). That happens when our actions are "good and right and true" (Ephesians 5:9).

While others ignore the beggar on the street and pass him by, Joan pauses, pulls out some loose change, smiles, and offers the money in a kind and friendly way. She often engages the person in conversation. Her act of charity toward a stranger is like a shooting star bringing a momentary streak of light from a different world—and others notice it.

Philip made the conscious decision to move beyond his anger and forgive the employee who had stolen two hundred dollars from the cash register. He also refused to fire the woman, knowing she was struggling to raise two children alone. Fifteen years later, Philip's son remembered this incident as he himself struggled with the possible decision to fire an employee. Some deeds of light have a long afterglow.

Tired though he is after a long forty-hour workweek, Eddie drives one hour every Saturday afternoon to visit his childhood buddy suffering from Alzheimer's disease. Mark lives in a silent, faraway world and is rarely able to communicate with, much less recognize, this stranger beside him. Nevertheless, Eddie is there every weekend. Patients and friends of the home stand in admiration of Eddie's selflessness and fidelity and often silently ponder how they themselves can be such faithful friends to others. Deeds of light often shoot sparks into the lives of others without our awareness.

Many famous and not-so-famous Christian charitable organizations were founded precisely to be beacons of light for those in material, spiritual, or mental darkness. For almost eighty years, Catholic Relief Services has been easing suffering, fostering charity, and preserving the dignity of human life in the lives of needy people regardless of their religion, race, or ethnicity. Founded in 1982, Food for the Poor provides food, housing, education, and medical care to seventeen of the poorest countries in the Caribbean, Mexico, Central America, and South America. Lifeline Christian Mission, founded by Bob and Gretchen Devoe, provides physical and spiritual care to needy people in Honduras, Cuba, and El Salvador. The Salvation Army provides hunger relief, housing assistance, homeless services, substance abuse rehabilitation, and prison ministries for people around the world. Founded in 1992, Advancing Native Missions trains and uses native members of a particular culture to spread the word of God to cultures that have little access to biblical resources and teachings. With the support of fourteen sponsor countries around the world, nearly two million babies, children, and young adults have been released from spiritual, economic, social, and physical poverty through Compassion International's Christ-centered, child-focused, church-based programs.

Practiced by individuals and organizations, the godly deeds of the Peace Prayer—love, forgiveness, consolation, understanding, and selfless charity—illumine a world often darkened by fears, attachments, the need to be in control, and a sense of entitlement. Such selfless deeds shed light on the practical consequences of walking in the footsteps of the Lord and Divine Master.

GOD AND OTHERS

Bob, a Franciscan priest, was an instrument of God's light who walked in the footsteps of the Lord and Divine Master in a very special way. He was one of the first Catholic priests to respond to the AIDS crisis in the mid-80s. Establishing a home in New Orleans for those living with the disease, he spent more than twenty years ministering to AIDS patients at Lazarus House.

One day, a bed-ridden resident asked about the crucifix Bob was wearing around his neck.

"It's called the San Damiano cross. It's a small replica of the crucifix that spoke to Saint Francis when he was struggling to figure out what God wanted him to do."

"And who are those five people standing alongside Jesus?"

"They are the five witnesses to the crucifixion. Here on Jesus's right side are his mother and John, the beloved disciple. Here on Jesus's left side are Mary Magdalene..."

"Mary Magdalene?" The patient interrupted Bob. "You mean, *the* Mary Magdalene? The former prostitute?"

"Why, yes."

"No one ever told me! I thought..."

Suspecting what he was going to say, Bob interrupted him. "The worst of sinners are the closest to Jesus's heart. That's why Mary Magdalene is right there next to him. Jesus forgives everyone who turns to him."

Tears streaming down his cheeks, the patient repeated, "I never knew. No one ever told me. I thought I was lost for good."

Bending over and hugging the patient, Bob said, "Oh, no. You're closer to him than you realize."

Bob's compassion and explanation gave the patient a new, brighter image of God that sustained him in the final weeks of his life.

The godly deeds of the Peace Prayer illumine a new portrait of God. In a world made gloomy by the image of a warrior God or a vengeful God or a picayune God, godly deeds are incarnations of "the Father of lights" (James 1:17). Helping the elderly neighbor with grocery shopping, accepting someone despite his or her lifestyle, deciding to recycle, valiantly ministering to the sick during a pandemic, contributing to a charitable organization, encouraging someone with a pat on the back, and refusing to strike back in violence all witness to how God uses his instruments and servants to express and reflect the divine care, concern, and compassion for creation. God is the source of all deeds of light, and his vibrant presence mysteriously glistens behind them.

Godly deeds also illumine the familial relationship we share with one another. We are family—brothers and sisters to one another. "But if we walk in the light as [Jesus] is in the light, then we have fellowship with one another..." (1 John 1:7). Following in the footsteps of the Lord and Divine Master is never a solitary affair.

In the Peace Prayer, we pray to sow light in the midst of darkness. That light comes from the flame of faith that has illumined our paths since the day of our baptism. The Peace Prayer reminds us to brighten the lives of others with deeds that manifest our familial bonds as children of a loving, forgiving God who, in the words of Francis of Assisi, is reflected in Brother Sun.

CUSTOMIZE YOUR TRAINING

- How does your faith affect the way you see the world? When has this vision been a source of consolation and encouragement for you? What world events or natural disasters have challenged your spiritual vision? Why?
- Reflect on the deeds of light you have seen others perform. How have they brightened your day and challenged you? What deeds of light do you deliberately practice?

··

SPIRITUAL COOLDOWN

Ponder

For once you were darkness, but now in the Lord you are light. Live as children of light—for the fruit of the light is found in all that is good and right and true. Try to find out what is pleasing to the Lord. Take no part in the unfruitful works of darkness, but instead expose them. (Ephesians 5:8–11)

Imitate

[Francis] was to be a light for those who believe that, by bearing witness of the light, he might prepare a way for the Lord to the hearts of his faithful, a way of light and peace. By the glorious splendor of his life and teaching Francis shone like the day-star amid the clouds, and by the brilliance which radiated from him he guided those who live in darkness, in the shadow of death, to the light. (Bonaventure, *Major Life of St. Francis*, Prologue, 1)

Pray

Lord and Divine Master, so kindle the fire of faith within me that I might illumine a world sometimes darkened by apathy, greed, and selfishness. Amen.

CHAPTER EIGHT

And Where There Is Sadness, Joy

Carol was a very successful, self-employed businesswoman for many years. Her success was on display in the first-class plane tickets and lodging in five-star hotels she enjoyed for her annual international vacations with her husband and two children. A staunch Catholic, she believed her success was a result of her walking in the footsteps of the Lord and Divine Master.

However, in May 2008, her lust for quick, easy money led her to make some large, risky investments. With the crash of the stock market that began in October of that year, she lost almost 75 percent of her savings.

For the next five years, she lived with a crushed spirit. She became obsessed with finances, especially the money she needed to support her two children studying in British universities. She was also despondent and depressed, feeling God had abandoned her and her family. Those feelings often drove her to the sofa where she would lie listless with wet, dull eyes staring at the ceiling.

THE SOURCES OF SADNESS

Many different factors can contribute to sadness and unhappiness. Some are physical: Sensitivity to light or the lack of it can lead to seasonal affective disorder, commonly known as SAD. Genetics, a chemical imbalance in the body, hormones, or a medical condition can make us melancholy. Television commercials remind us that certain medications can affect our moods, as can our diet and sleep habits. With a change of routine or the proper medical attention, these sources can often be addressed and cease being an obstacle or hindrance to our emotional well-being.

Current events can overwhelm our outlook and moods, pulling us down and making us feel sad. The COVID-19 pandemic of 2020 instilled fear and weighed heavily on the hearts of many people. The plight of refugees, the sudden deaths of innocent schoolchildren, the loss of a love, the failed job interview, the struggle with finances, or even the defeat in a ball game can affect how we feel today. From the tragic to the trivial, some incidents raise more questions than answers that often lead to brooding and flirting with gloom.

Sadness is Amanda's knee-jerk reaction to unpleasant situations that remind her she doesn't always get what she wants, and she is not the master of her own destiny. "I'm doing everything correctly. So why isn't life cooperating with me?" she rhetorically asks. Sometimes she's down in the dumps for an afternoon. Sometimes a season.

Like Amanda, we too can become sad in situations that demand we loosen our grip on life. In sickness and job loss and death, when confronted with our inability to be in control of a situation, we often ask in grief and regret, "Why doesn't God help?"

And it's not just the loss of control—the loss of a personality prop or an attachment like an automobile or pet, insignificant to others as it may be in the grand scheme of things, can bring on a season of sorrow as well.

I'm prone to heartache over indifference. When I find myself shaking my head because someone is apathetic, insensitive, or uninterested in my needs, my first reaction is to dwell on my sense of entitlement and ask, "Why doesn't he care? Doesn't she see I need help?" Those questions also arise when I see others being indifferent to situations that I hold close to my heart; I get thrown for a loop when I witness someone being nonchalant, lukewarm, or unresponsive to the sufferings of others, especially the victims of natural disasters.

Sadness lurks and loiters around disappointment. When high hopes and tingling expectations suddenly crash into reality, our instant reaction is "Why?" Disappointments can drain us of our color and jeopardize our sure footing, causing us to slip into a potential ditch of despair.

"BABYLONIAN STUFF"

In 587 B.C., the Israelites experienced a great national tragedy that pushed them to the brink of despair. Jerusalem was conquered and destroyed, many Israelites were killed, and even more were sent into exile in Babylon. For almost fifty years, they would be disoriented as they lived outside the Promised Land, without the Temple, and seemingly without God's presence. Psalm 137 captures the grief and sorrow of this event:

> By the rivers of Babylon—
>> there we sat down and there we wept
>> when we remembered Zion.
> On the willows there
>> we hung up our harps,
> For there our captors
>> asked us for songs,
> and our tormentors asked for mirth, saying,
>> "Sing us one of the songs of Zion!" (vv. 1–3)

Francis of Assisi rightly calls sadness the "Babylonian stuff"[35] and blames it on the devil. The saint says the devil carries dust "so that he can throw it into even the tiniest chinks of conscience and soil the candor of mind and purity of life."[36] How many times have I found myself dwelling on past sins confessed long ago? Those times dampen my mood. How many times do I fixate on inappropriate mental images or fidget with physical temptations? Both are examples of the devil fiddling with my conscience, mind, or life and trying to throw his dust in it. Such experiences can make me suddenly feel ill at ease, disoriented, and like a stranger. I am exiled from the familiar, the known, the expected, and the good—I'm in Babylon.

In such situations, Francis insists I must not allow the devil to take away my joy of spirit and my holy cheerfulness. If Satan does, I might be prone to acedia, one of the deadly sins, that causes me to fall into the trap of "vain enjoyments,"[37] turning my back on the Lord and Divine Master and seeking superficial pleasures to ease the pain, find comfort, and grope in the dark for a way home. If this is not addressed, Francis says the devil's sadness will gradually produce "abiding rust in the heart."[38]

Though couched in a medieval understanding of the spiritual life, this is extraordinarily wise and contemporary advice. How often do I seek empty enjoyment and attempt to self-medicate so I don't feel sadness or depression? Instead of confronting the sources of my sadness, I pull the curtain over them and suppress them by turning to inappropriate behaviors to distract myself and make myself feel better. Sadly, modern medical science reminds me that this kind of response can lay the foundation for addiction, the abiding rust referred to by Francis.

TRUE AND PERFECT JOY

It's not just the wiles, tricks, and machinations of the devil that can get us down. Francis reminds us that sometimes we can be our own worst enemy.

One of the early friars, Brother Leonard, narrates how Saint Francis taught Brother Leo, his close friend and confessor, an important spiritual lesson about true and perfect joy.

"Brother Leo," Francis said, "I want you to write this down. Let's say we receive word that all the professors at the University of Paris have decided to follow in the footsteps of the Lord and Divine Master and enter our way of life. Write down: this is not true joy!

"And let's say all the hierarchy—the cardinals, archbishops, and bishops—from beyond the northern mountains as well as the kings of France and England have decided to follow our way of life. Write it clearly: this is not true joy!"

Francis continued by stating true joy wasn't in the friars converting all the nonbelievers to the Christian faith or even he himself suddenly developing the ability to heal the sick or do other miracles.

Shaking his head in bewilderment, Brother Leo asked, "What then is true joy?"

"It's midnight," Francis replied, "and I'm just returning to the Portiuncula after walking from Perugia. It's wintertime and I'm all muddy and dirty. Icicles have formed on my habit and keep striking my legs, making them bloody. I get to the gate, knock, and then yell to wake someone up. A brother comes and asks, 'Who are you?' I tell him it's me. And he replies, 'Get out of here! You shouldn't be out so late. You can't come in!' When I press him on it, he continues by saying, 'I said, go away! You're a fool. You're stupid. There's too many of us like you here. Go away!' I stand my ground and humbly say, 'For the love of God, please let me in.' And he replies, 'Absolutely not. Go to the Crosiers' place and maybe they'll take you in.'

"I tell you, Brother Leo. If I had patience and didn't become upset, this would not only be true joy but also true virtue and the salvation of my soul."

This teaching of Saint Francis can be mined on three levels. First, it occurs at St. Mary of the Little Portion ("Portiuncula"), the small chapel in the valley outside Assisi that was given to Francis by the Benedictines. Francis considered it the womb of the Order, and it was his most beloved place. His imagined rejection at this very place speaks volumes about his sense of detachment and his walking in the footsteps of the Lord and Divine Master. Like Jesus who emptied himself and didn't have a place to lay his head (see Luke 9:58), Francis doesn't cling to the right of having a place to call home—not even at his beloved Portiuncula. We can sometimes be our own source of sadness when we tightly clench our fists and refuse to let go of our attachments.

Second, Francis's hypothetical self-description of being muddy, dirty, and bloody is reminiscent of the lepers, the societal outcasts and marginalized of his day. The saint's early conversion was centered precisely on ministering to them—at the end of his life in his Testament, he specifically mentioned his encounter with them as an expression of the gratuity of grace. The fact that Francis imagines the brothers of the Portiuncula treating and rejecting him as a leper is indicative of a sad development in the Order. Those whom Francis is remembered as once calling "brothers in Christ"[39] are now considered by the friars, as most medieval people had considered them, outcasts and unwelcomed. We can sometimes be our own source of sadness when we fear or fight change and insist on maintaining control of what worked in the past.

Third, Francis identifies himself to the brother who comes to the door. The brother certainly knew him to be the founder, and yet he calls Francis a stupid fool. As head of the Order, the saint refused to exercise his rightful authority over the brother. We can sometimes be our own source of sadness when we insist on our sense of entitlement.

The story teaches an important lesson. By refusing to allow his centripetal attachments, control needs, and sense of entitlement to hold sway over himself, Francis was able to maintain his peace and joy. The secret to his joy is detachment from the ego. We can sometimes be our own source of happiness when we respond to the gratuity of grace and train our souls to move from selfishness to selflessness.

HERALD OF THE GREAT KING

This detachment from the ego can be seen in a vignette from chapter 7 of the first biography of Francis.

In the days following the renunciation of his inheritance and clothes before his father, the bishop, and the townspeople of Assisi, Francis, singing praises to God in French, his mother's maiden tongue, would roam the countryside and forests. One day, while in a forest, bandits attacked him.

"Just who do you think you are?" they demanded.

"I am the Herald of the great King! How about that?" he replied.

The bandits seized him, threw him in a snow-filled ditch, and retorted, "Well, then, lie there, you stupid Herald of God!"

After they left, the future saint rolled around, shook the snow off himself, jumped out of the ditch, and continued on his way.

The biographer concludes, "[G]lad with great joy, he began to call out the praises of God in a loud voice throughout the grove."[40]

For Francis, training the soul in the service of the Master included distancing oneself from the demands of the ego, prone as it is for retaliation and revenge. This is how the saint preserved his cheerfulness and joy.

REJOICE ALWAYS

Despite the reality of sadness in our lives, the New Testament letters admonish us to "rejoice in the Lord always" (Philippians 4:4)—even during times of suffering and tribulation (see 1 Peter 4:13) as seen in the preceding vignette from the life of Francis. Following the biblical mandate, the saint even commands that the friars "should let it be seen that they are happy in God, cheerful and courteous, as is expected of them, and be careful not to appear gloomy or depressed like hypocrites."[41]

But how do we sow the seeds of joy in the midst of our own or another's sadness and disappointments? To return to the words of Psalm 137, "How could we sing the Lord's song in a foreign land?" (v. 4). How can we train the soul to distance itself from a bruised ego? An incident from the life of the Lord and Divine Master provides the direction for finding our way out of Babylon and rediscovering our joy.

The Gospel of John records an awkward, intimate moment in the life of Jesus—weeping at the death of his friend Lazarus (11:35)—watched publicly by the crowd. Judging from the crowd's reaction, Jesus's grief must have been great, "See how much he loved him!" (v. 36). However, rather than bringing him down to prolonged, self-centered sadness and depression, this event drove Jesus to pray with a confidence unmatched by most of us. "Father, I thank you for having heard me. I knew that you always hear me…" (vv. 41–42). Therein lies the secret to sowing seeds of joy in the midst of sadness.

When confronted with a situation that could have consumed him with sorrow and sadness, Jesus looked beyond himself and focused on the God whom he had freely chosen to serve. He moved from a centripetal to a centrifugal stance. He approached God with a distinctive prayer. Rather than trying to change God's will or force the hand of God, Jesus prayed with the confidence and assurance that every aspiration of the human heart and every prayer are heard. This confidence lifted him above his sadness and grief and led him in the direction toward home.

THE LORD IS MY SHEPHERD

This is the secret to Vincent's happiness. I was reminded of that in a conversation I had with him in mainland China more than twenty-five years ago. He had come to China to recoup the family savings lost by the collapse of the Argentine economy. After fifteen painful months of trying to negotiate deals, Vincent still had not earned the financial resources to bring his wife and two daughters to China.

He told me over dinner one night, "People must think I am crazy. Though I still haven't earned a nickel, nevertheless, I am completely optimistic, upbeat, and hopeful. Actually, I am happy! Every night as I go to sleep, I pray Psalm 23.

> The Lord is my shepherd, I shall not want…
> Even though I walk through the darkest valley,
> I fear no evil;
> for you are with me;
> your rod and your staff—
> they comfort me.

"After praying that psalm slowly and deliberately, I can sleep soundly. It reminds me that when life pushes me into a corner, I have the best possible defense—the will of God! So I need to let go of my desires. I surrender. And then I just trust."

Gesticulating with a lit cigar in his hand as if he were leading a seminar on how to invest money according to biblical principles, he added, "After all, when all is said and done, *Mon Père,*"— this Argentinian always mistakenly thought I understood French because of the French pronunciation of my first name—"the events of the universe and my little life are both in God's hands. It's up to God to decide how they should come together."

With the cigar smoke clearing over our dessert, Vincent paused and then added, "When we can't trace God's finger in an event, then all we can do is trust God's heart."

Vincent convinced me that joy is the sign that one is walking in the footsteps of the Lord and Divine Master. No wonder Francis referred to sad and gloomy friars as hypocrites—highlighting the word's Greek etymology as "stage actor, pretender, dissembler." Joy is not a costume we wear or a feeling we fake; it is the foundation of our lives. It comes from training the soul to catch the Spirit's selfless, centrifugal force, fixing our glance outward, upward, with a prayer of confidence while keeping our feet firmly on the ground in service and surrender to God.

Cause of Our Joy

Christian joy is not simply a superficial feeling of heightened delight or the emotion accompanying extreme pleasure. It does not necessarily depend upon one's immediate circumstances or fortune as taught by Saint Francis's example. As Vincent gives witness, it does not ignore or deny the troubling reality of indifference, hopelessness, or disappointment.

Christian joy lies beyond the realm of feelings and emotions. It is a fundamental disposition and stance toward life. Descriptive metaphors for it abound: It is the knowledge that having prayed and surrendered, God hears the hopes and desires of my heart and will respond in a timely, appropriate way. God is my shepherd and I must trust God's heart. Joy feeds on the fact that God stands watch over every situation in my life and guides me with rod and staff. My joy sometimes bubbles up, sometimes surges up, from the rock-bottom certainty that the finger of God is somehow present in every tragic or trivial event. Joy is the oasis residing in the confident conviction that the waters of God's loving care and concern never run dry—not even in the desert. The gratuity of grace is always unending and never expiring. Joy is rooted in the reality of a stone door rolled back from its tomb.

Sowing seeds of joy amid sadness requires the two fundamentals of soul training: prayer—invoking assurance and confidence that God is looking out for us—and action—a servant's surrender and acceptance of consequences without clinging to fears, attachments, control needs, and a sense of entitlement. Both prayer and action plant a servant's feet in the footprints that lead beyond the tomb of Lazarus and the cross of Calvary.

CUSTOMIZE YOUR TRAINING

- This chapter mentioned a few sources of sadness: physical factors, certain events, deflated hopes, apathetic indifference, lack of control, and disappointment. What are the primary sources of sadness for you? How do you retain your joy in the midst of them?

- Francis of Assisi taught that true joy comes when we let go of our fears of change, our attachments, our control needs, and our sense of entitlement. How do you maintain your joy when your fears, attachments, control needs, and sense of entitlement are threatened? What helps you grow in a spirit of detachment?

SPIRITUAL COOLDOWN

Ponder
Blessed are those who mourn, for they will be comforted. (Matthew 5:4)

Imitate

Francis once saw a certain companion of his with a peevish and sad face, and not taking this lightly, he said to him: "It is not becoming for a servant of God to show himself sad or upset before men, but always he should show himself honorable. Examine your offenses in your room and weep and groan before your God. When you return to your brothers, put off your sorrow and conform yourself to the rest." And after a few more things he said: "They who are jealous of the salvation of men envy me greatly; they are always trying to disturb in my companions what they cannot disturb in me." So much, however, did he love a man who was full of spiritual joy that he had these words written down as an admonition to all at a certain general chapter: "Let the brothers beware lest they show themselves outwardly gloomy and sad hypocrites; but let them show themselves joyful in the Lord, cheerful and suitably gracious." (Thomas of Celano, *The Second Life of Saint Francis*, 128)

Pray

Lord and Divine Master, may your grace free me from my selfishness so that I may be an instrument of infectious joy for the sorrowful and burdened. Amen.

CHAPTER NINE

Grant that I May Not So Much Seek to Be Consoled as to Console; to Be Understood as to Understand; to Be Loved as to Love

Peter felt sorry for himself because he didn't get the promotion. Absorbed in his disappointment and searching for sympathy, he told everyone at work. His colleagues, weary of his complaining, bristled and started to avoid him after a few days.

Susan knew her friends thought she had been impatient and unreasonable at the restaurant. So she telephoned each of them individually to justify her actions and defend what she had said to the waitress. Each thought her phone call was making a mountain out of a molehill.

Allison had gone through three boyfriends in nine months. She was frustrated because she could not find someone to take care of her and give her a comfortable life. She was, in fact, not looking for love at all but for another father to cater to her needs.

A BLACK HOLE

We Westerners, and Americans in particular, are overly attentive and accommodating to our own desires, wants, needs, and wishes. The centripetal force is engrained within us. Just count the number of times you say, "I, me, and mine" to see your selfishness. Count the number of your self-centered social media posts.

We think the world should revolve around ourselves and, much to the consternation of others, mistakenly think all our Facebook friends and Twitter followers are interested in every single detail of our daily lives.

I once heard a friend describe his brother as "a bloated, self-centered black hole that sucks all light, and everything else, into himself. He's literally stuck on himself and has a knack for dragging everyone nearby into his darkness." That description could also describe many of us as well as Peter, Susan, and Allison. Focused on the self, some want to be consoled, others understood, and still others loved.

Jesus portrays the elder brother in the parable of the prodigal son (Luke 15:11–32) as a kind of black hole. Adamant about being understood, he was unwilling to try to understand the cause of his father's joy. His self-absorption, self-pity, and need to be appreciated and consoled apparently hindered him from attending the family reunion. Needy, self-absorbed people have a way of isolating themselves and making their presence felt by their absence.

How do we break out of the isolation and constricting limitations of the ego's centripetal pull into a self-centered world? How do we resist becoming a black hole? It requires a change in our thinking as radical and revolutionary as that of Copernicus.

CHANGE THE CENTER OF GRAVITY

The second half of the Peace Prayer trains the soul in the centrifugal force that shifts the center of gravity and our attention away from ourselves to others. We do this by practicing the three traditional forms of empathy: cognitive, emotional, and compassionate.[42]

Cognitive empathy seeks to intellectually understand the other person's feelings, thinking, and perspective on a situation. "I'm just trying to get inside your head and understand your take on this," as a friend often tells me. When we seek to understand rather than be understood, our world expands as we become aware of and sometimes comfortable with diverse viewpoints. With such knowledge, we can attempt to motivate others to respond to a situation in a way they might otherwise not. This is what the father of the prodigal son attempted but apparently failed to succeed in doing with his older son: "Son, you are always with me, and all that is mine is yours. But we had to celebrate and rejoice, because this brother of yours was dead and has come to life; he was lost and has been found" (Luke 15:31–32). If there is any pitfall to cognitive empathy, it's that an intellectual understanding, without putting ourselves in others' shoes and feeling what they feel, can be insufficient, making us come across as insensitive, aloof, and unfeeling.

Emotional empathy goes deeper than cognitive empathy and challenges us to emotionally connect with other people. When we seek to console rather than be consoled, we put ourselves in others' shoes, imagine ourselves as them, and allow their situation to pull at our heartstrings. Think again of the prodigal son parable: The father, seeing his younger son coming down the road and feeling his embarrassment, shame, and disgrace, was "filled with compassion" (v. 20). He ran out to meet his son, embraced him, and showered him with symbols of affection and acceptance. A consequence of emotional empathy is that the gut reaction and visceral response to a situation need to be managed appropriately, as they can be overwhelming to the more sensitive person. Without proper management, the emotional response can lead to exhaustion, fatigue, and ultimately burnout.

Compassionate empathy marries cognitive and emotional empathy and gives birth to action. When we decide to love rather than be loved, we are compelled to respond and help the person in need. We consider the person's entire situation and attempt to comfort the person by emotionally sharing what the person is feeling and improving the situation in whatever way we can. Sometimes this can be as simple and powerful as being present and accompanying the person in suffering. Think of Job's three friends who, hearing of Job's suffering, sought him out and sat in silence with him for seven days and seven nights (Job 2:13). Compassionate empathy always brings a mindful, sympathetic presence and sometimes an action for change.

Francis and a 'Dying' Friar

An event in the early life of the Franciscan community highlights Saint Francis's practice of this virtue.

The first friars were sharing close quarters in an abandoned hut at Rivo Torto. In the middle of the night, one of the brothers started yelling, "I'm dying! I'm dying!" Startled and frightened, the brothers woke up.

Getting up and lighting a lamp, Francis asked who was yelling. Discovering who the brother was, he asked why he thought he was dying.

"I'm dying of hunger," the brother replied and admitted he had been fasting excessively.

Francis did not want the brother to feel ashamed. So he immediately set the table and invited all the brothers to sit for a meal.

Upon finishing their meal, Francis reminded the brothers that each person has a different constitution. "Some people need more food while others need less. We must provide for the body according to its constitution. Not only must we be careful to overindulge, we must also be careful of excessive fasting and abstinence because, as the Bible says, the Lord desires mercy and not sacrifice.

"Brothers, charity and necessity compelled me to have each of us share a meal with our brother so that he wouldn't be embarrassed to eat alone. But for the future, let's all remember: each of us should properly provide for the needs of the body without overindulgence or underindulgence."[43]

In an age when fasting was considered a necessary sacrifice for soul training, Francis reminded the brothers that mercy toward the body and one's neighbor takes precedence. This is compassionate empathy in action.

THE DETAILS OF COMPASSION

Unlike Saint Francis, we are sometimes helpless and unable to change or improve a person's situation. Father Ralph, a contemporary follower of Francis with whom I lived for two years, has an extraordinary gift for compassionate empathy and taught me so much about it. Watching him console a college student who just had been rejected by his girlfriend or talk with the friary cook who was angry about something was always a lesson in selflessness and humility for me. No situation was ever too trivial for Ralph. I once asked him about his gift and, after initially blushing, he offered some practical and insightful tips for training the soul in compassionate empathy.

"Albert, empathy starts with putting yourself in the other's shoes and feeling what the person is feeling. This can be a challenge especially when you have never experienced what the person is experiencing—sometimes you must look for an analogous situation in your own life. It's critical to try to feel the other's distress or disappointment. Without compassion, your consolation, understanding, or love is simply a cosmetic whitewash.

"You have to be sensitive to your tone of voice, your body language, and the words you speak. You certainly don't want to come across as condescending to the hurting person. Acknowledge your connection to the person's pain, feeble as it may be, and validate that person's feelings by saying something like, 'I am so sorry to hear about this. I know that game, that person, that promotion—whatever—was important to you.' By doing that, you break the person's feelings of loneliness and isolation."

Ralph went on to advise against any attempt at humor—"That can feel uncaring, flippant, and cruel to the person"—and any attempt to cheer the person up or put a positive spin on the situation—"'Look on the bright side' or 'You watch, something good will come of this' are not words a person wants to hear initially." He reminded me to never belittle the person's disappointment.

"Encourage the person to delve more deeply into the feelings of hurt and disappointment with statements like, 'It's so unfair, isn't it?' 'This must really anger you.' 'How do you manage to cope?' Then just listen. Don't be afraid of silence as the person searches to express deeper feelings and maybe even memories from the past. If you're at a loss for words, admit it, and never be afraid to say, 'I have no idea how this must make you feel, but I do care for you so much.' Honesty is better than a smoke screen of compassion. And I've learned that when it's appropriate, a physical sign of affection can be quite helpful: a pat on the back, a hand on the shoulder, or a hug can go a long way in helping someone feel consoled, understood, and loved. Touch is often more powerful than words. It can help lead the person to a place of emotional healing."

Ralph's advice made it clear to me that compassionate empathy does not come naturally or by osmosis. Rather, the soul must be trained in it.

THE EXAMPLE OF JESUS
The Lord and Divine Master's compassionate empathy was on display in the village of Nain. Arriving at the village gate, Jesus

encountered a funeral procession (see Luke 7:11–17). A young man, the only son of his widowed mother, had died. Having lost not only her husband but also her son, the woman would have been rendered penniless since the sources of her financial support were dead. As a woman, she would have been unable to inherit any property. She was now dependent on the charity of her distant relatives and friends. Having "compassion for her" (v. 13), Jesus approached the funeral bier, raised the son from the dead, and gave him back to his mother. This gift of Jesus's compassionate empathy returned not only the woman's son but also her financial stability.

Here's another example from the life of Jesus. At his time, there was nothing more dreaded than the disease of leprosy. The disease was a sentence to a subhuman existence. Not only badly disfiguring a person, leprosy rendered people unfit for life among others and unclean for public worship. It drove people into the desert where they lived alone and apart from the rest of society. Lepers were the "untouchables," for to touch a leper was to render oneself ritually impure and put oneself at risk of contracting the contagious disease.

One day, a leper violated the social and religious norms by approaching Jesus (see Mark 1:40–45). No doubt the sheer desperation of his loneliness, as well as the human need to be touched by another, drove him to the feet of Jesus, where he begged to be healed. Most people naturally would have become self-centered and self-conscious if an untouchable approached them so boldly and brazenly as this leper. But Jesus clearly understood the pain of the leper's disease and isolation. "Moved with pity" (v. 41)—a gospel phrase suggesting the deepest pangs of compassionate empathy—Jesus responded to the leper's request with an action that matched the boldness of the leper's: before healing him, Jesus rendered himself ritually impure and risked contraction of the disease by stretching out his hand and touching the leper.

The touch of Jesus was not simply a healing touch. It was also a touch of consolation, understanding, and love. Jesus moved beyond himself and what should have been his self-concerns about purity and health. He focused his attention on the need of the leper. The touch of Jesus brought the leper back into society and, more important, into a one-to-one relationship that the leper had previously not known. One could suggest that this was more meaningful—and more surprising—than the actual physical healing.

Time and again, Jesus modeled for his followers the centrifugal attitude of compassionate empathy expressed in selfless surrender, self-denying sacrifice, and solicitous service toward others:

- "Father, if you are willing, remove this cup from me; yet, not my will but yours be done" (Luke 22:42).
- "But I say to you that listen, Love your enemies, do good to those who hate you, bless those who curse you, pray for those who abuse you" (Luke 6:27–28).
- "The greatest among you will be your servant" (Matthew 23:11).
- "For the Son of Man came not to be served but to serve, and to give his life a ransom for many" (Mark 10:45).

Instruments of God walk in the footsteps of the Lord and Divine Master when they put flesh and bones on this spirit of kenotic selflessness. That is the secret not only to compassionate empathy but also to consolation, understanding, and love.

ANOTHER LEPER

Francis of Assisi walked in these footsteps. Like most medieval people, the future saint was repulsed by the sight of lepers. He might have mistakenly believed he encountered them more often than he actually did since the Hospital Brothers of Saint Anthony ran a hospital located down in the valley outside the walls of Assisi for victims of Saint Anthony's Fire, a gangrenous disease sometimes confused with leprosy.

One day, after being released from the prison in Perugia, Francis came face-to-face with the dreaded disease. In a rare moment of grace, his internal center of gravity shifted from the centripetal to the centrifugal. He recalled the experience at the end of his life in his Testament:

> This is how God inspired me, Brother Francis, to embark upon a life of penance. When I was in sin, the sight of lepers nauseated me beyond measure; but then God himself led me into their company, and I had pity on them. When I had once become acquainted with them, what had previously nauseated me became a source of spiritual and physical consolation for me. After that I did not wait long before leaving the world.[44]

This encounter and Francis's response to the gratuity of grace had a profound impact on his soul training. His compassionate empathy transformed his visceral reaction to lepers and gave him the ability to see and touch the holy in the hideous. This provided the impetus to begin walking in the footsteps of the Lord and Divine Master—what Francis referred to, in the parlance of his day, as "leaving the world."

This encounter also might have had a terminal impact on his soul training. Two medical professionals have suggested that at the end of his life, Francis might have suffered from clinically significant leprosy of the borderline or tuberculoid form.[45] Had this radical act of compassionate empathy in his early life transformed Francis in his later life into one of the very marginalized to whom he ministered? Had his life come full circle? If so, his self-less response to the lepers is a stunning indication of how God's grace was transforming him into the image of the Lord and Divine Master who himself had identified with society's marginalized and outcast (see Matthew 25:31–46).

In three simple verses, the Peace Prayer gets to the crux of what it means to train the soul in compassionate empathy. It is following the centrifugal force of the Spirit that leads us to walk in the footsteps of the Lord and Divine Master by living a life of kenotic selflessness through selfless surrender, self-denying sacrifice, and solicitous service. In so doing, we show how the gratuity of grace, never exhausted and never expiring, is incarnated in God's instruments.

Customize Your Training

- Do you naturally incline toward cognitive, emotional, or compassionate empathy? What practices can strengthen your soul training to help you become more consoling, understanding, and loving?
- Whom do you consider to be lepers among your family, acquaintances, and society? How can you become more compassionately empathetic in your relationship with them?

Spiritual Cooldown

Ponder

Do nothing from selfish ambition or conceit, but in humility regard others as better than yourselves. Let each of you look not to your own interests, but to the interests of others. (Philippians 2:3–4)

Imitate

Francis sympathized lovingly and compassionately with those stricken with any physical affliction and he immediately referred to Christ the poverty or deprivation he saw in anyone. He was kind and gentle by nature and the love of Christ merely intensified this. His soul melted at the sight of the poor or infirm and when he could not offer material assistance he lavished his affection. (Bonaventure, *The Major Legend of Saint Francis*, 8:5)

Pray

Lord and Divine Master, may I imitate you by surrendering to the Father's will, sacrificing my selfish desires, and serving my brothers and sisters in need. Amen.

CHAPTER TEN

For It Is in Giving that We Receive

One day, I was depressed and discouraged. I decided to take a walk through Tiananmen Square. I hoped the fresh air, the kite flyers, and the hundreds of Chinese who stroll through the square every day would perk me up.

I saw an elderly beggar. His weather-beaten face, unkempt hair, wrinkled clothes, and dirty appearance were sure signs that he, like others one encounters in Beijing, had come from the countryside and had spent at least a few days living on the street.

He approached me with an outstretched hand. I hesitated and stared into his eyes as he continuously muttered, "*Xiansheng, dui bu qi*"(Sir, excuse me). In those needy eyes, I saw hundreds of missed opportunities, the pain of the Cultural Revolution, a life in the countryside with squat toilets and no running water, and the humiliation of begging. With the grace of generosity suddenly welling up inside of me, I opened my wallet and pulled out a ten yuan note (about $1.20 at the time), a very generous offering by Chinese standards. He waved it off and, pointing to a five yuan note, said, "*Gou le*" (That's enough).

As I handed him the five yuan, my mood lifted. My soul was flooded with light as I received a toothless smile as wide as the Great Wall and as bright as that day's midmorning sun.

The Peace Prayer hits the nail on the head: it truly is in giving that we receive.

THE CONTAGION OF CHARITY

That experience is certainly not unique to me. We've all had the experience of watching a sacrifice or gift come back to us in ways beyond all telling.

Parents, teachers, people in the helping profession, and volunteers all know the tremendous satisfaction that comes when someone's gratitude outbids the paycheck. Those who follow in the footsteps of the Lord and Divine Master by training their souls to be generous to others are rewarded in a multitude of ways. And sometimes the centrifugal force of charity can be contagious.

For many years, some contemporary Scripture scholars suggested that may have been behind John's version of the miracle of the feeding of the five thousand. This is the only miracle found in all four Gospels (Matthew 14:13–21; Mark 6:31–44; Luke 9:12–17; John 6:1–14). A large crowd had followed Jesus up a mountain and, as was the custom, the majority would not have wandered far from town without bringing along some food. When it was time to eat, Jesus questioned Philip about where to purchase some food for the crowd. Philip made it clear that even six months' wages would be insufficient to buy enough food for everyone (John 6:7). In the Fourth Gospel's version of the miracle, Andrew mentioned a boy with five barley loaves and two fish but quickly acknowledged, "But what are they among so many people?" (v. 9) The boy's simple and spontaneous offering, blessed by Jesus, must have shamed those who secretly held and hoarded the food they had brought with them. Seeing the boy's generosity, these people suddenly caught the contagion of his charity and shared their food with those who had not brought along some food. In a Gospel that often refers to a person's name or nationality, the boy's anonymity heightened the virtue of his act. The twelve baskets of leftovers are a symbol of the abundance of what is received by those who sacrifice and share what they have with others.

The Lord and Divine Master's blessing of the boy's gifts assures us that no gift—money, forgiveness, a listening ear, a minute of one's valuable time—will go unrecognized. "And whoever gives even a cup of cold water to one of these little ones in the name of a disciple—truly I tell you, none of these will lose their reward" (Matthew 10:42). It is a promise of the Lord that every time we give, we will, in fact, receive.

So Many Choices

A question often arises: who gets my donation? Every year, especially around Christmas, we are inundated with requests. Just this week, I received requests for money from a Poor Clare monastery, a Jesuit mission school for Native Americans, the American Cancer Society, a national shrine in honor of Saint Jude, and a Christian organization that sponsors needy children in Peru. I clearly understand Marge's predicament when she asked me in a spiritual direction session, "I would be broke if I answered each and every request. With so many choices, how do I decide who gets my contribution?"

"Here's what I do," I responded. "Over the years, I've developed a relationship with a charitable organization that helps the poor of St. Louis pay their water and electric bills. It's called the Franciscan Connection. I've visited the place once and have gotten to know the two friars who run it. So every few months, I donate a part of my monthly allowance to it. Around Christmas, depending on how my interest in piqued, I might challenge myself to make a one-time donation to just one other organization. And occasionally, in the case of natural disasters like hurricanes or tornadoes, I might respond to the request of Catholic Charities.

I cannot respond to every single request I get—but I can respond to one."

I suggested to Marge that she find herself a pet project or a charitable organization that spoke to her heart and let it become the target of her prayer and generosity. That becomes a practical way for her to train her soul in the centrifugal force of charity.

The Widow's Mite

Liberty Weekend occurred July 3–6, 1986, and celebrated the centenary of the Statue of Liberty on Liberty Island in New York with its $39 million restoration. Watching the reopening festivities on television, my mother glowed with pride as she announced, "My dollar donation helped make today possible!" I instantly thought of another widow whom Jesus himself noticed.

Sitting opposite the Temple's treasury, a gathering place for many Jews, Jesus watched people as they made their contributions. He noted how the wealthy put in sizable donations. But he singled out a poor widow whose contribution amounted to a penny. Calling his disciples, he said to them, "Truly I tell you, this poor widow has put in more than all those who are contributing to the treasury. For all of them have contributed out of their abundance; but she out of her poverty has put in everything she had, all she had to live on" (Mark 12:43–44).

Jesus is not criticizing the wealthy for their contributions. Their generous donations were no doubt appreciated. But what Jesus is lauding is the enormity of the woman's meager donation. As a widow who relied upon the generosity of family and neighbors for her living expenses, she no doubt felt the sting of her contribution of two copper coins.

Don't miss the point that Jesus is making: the important thing is not *how much* you give but *that* you give, that you share what you have with others.

The Treasures of the Church

Tradition says a Roman consul once called Saint Lawrence the Deacon for a meeting. He said to Lawrence, "The Empire right now is in dire financial straits. We need money. You followers of Christ have so many valuable treasures in your churches. I have seen your gold cups and silver candlesticks. I order you to give immediately all the precious treasures of your church to me for the benefit of the Empire."

Lawrence surprisingly agreed but said he would need one week to gather them all up. The consul approved of the requested delay.

A week later, Lawrence came before the consul again. The consul was surprised that Lawrence was not carrying any bags filled with the church's wealth.

"Where are the treasures I demanded you to bring to me?" "Sir," Lawrence replied, "they are so many that I had to leave them outside. But if you would follow me, I will gladly show them to you."

The consul immediately stood up and eagerly followed Lawrence out of the door. As they walked outside, the consul saw poor people, widows, orphans, lepers, the blind, the lame, and the sick.

With great pride and affection, Lawrence made a sweeping motion with his hand and said, "These, sir, are the treasures of my church!"

And treasures they are! Jesus consecrated them as divine tabernacles in his daily association and close identification with them. "Truly, I tell you, just as you did it to one of the least of these who are members of my family, you did it to me" (Matthew 25:40). Perhaps it is a grace and blessing that the poor will always be among us (see Mark 14:7). Their persistent presence allows those who walk in the footsteps of the Lord and Divine Master to train their souls daily in the practice of selfless surrender, self-denying sacrifice, and solicitous service. The journey of the Lord and Divine Master leads to the periphery of society where the poor, the exiled, and the ostracized reside. This is the womb of Christian spirituality and the birthplace of kenotic selflessness.

NEEDING THE POOR

Father Hugh was appointed to be the provincial (religious superior) in Taiwan of the Congregation of the Mission, a religious community founded in 1625 by Saint Vincent de Paul. Arriving in Taipei in the early 1990s, he immediately set about getting to know his confreres and studying Chinese. I was amazed at how well he quickly adapted to his new environment.

One day, about four months after he had arrived, I asked him how he was adjusting to life in the Far East.

"Albert, I've really amazed myself this time. Even though I'm in my early sixties, I haven't found this transfer as difficult as I thought it was going to be. Everyone has been so welcoming, accepting, and understanding.

"But you know," he continued, "there's just one thing that I really miss in my life right now."

My curiosity was piqued. Could it be Cheerios at breakfast? A bottle of scotch at a reasonable price?

"What's that?" I finally asked.

"The poor!" he replied with a fervor and intensity that I had not encountered since meeting him. "I miss not having a poor person in my life. At every other assignment, I've always managed to have a poor person in my life to help keep me in touch with the things that really matter. But there just doesn't seem to be any poor people around here. So I've decided to ask God to send a poor person into my life. I really need one."

It didn't take God long to answer Hugh's prayers. Within a matter of weeks, a man started hanging around the parish asking for handouts. I often saw Hugh sitting with him, talking to him, and sometimes reaching into his pocket, opening his wallet, and giving him some money. Before long, the man started calling the parish asking for Hugh at all hours of the day and night. Hugh always obliged to answer the man's phone calls.

After a couple of weeks, it became evident to Hugh that the man had a mild mental disorder. Sometimes he became abusive toward Hugh. Hugh tried to get the man some psychological help and a permanent place to sleep at night, but the man refused.

I still remember one evening Hugh got off the phone with the man, turned to me, and said, "You know, I prayed for a poor person in my life. God answered my prayer. And now, frankly, I just don't know what to do with him!"

"Can't you just tell him, 'Enough is enough,' and say you're not going to help anymore? You just might be wasting your time," I replied.

I could see the disappointment in his eyes. "I guess you just don't get it. I really need poor people in my life. Strange as it sounds, they actually enrich it."

Of course, the treasures of the Church are not always as psychologically healthy or honest and sincere as we would like them to be. We've all had the experience of meeting mentally ill street people who flatly refuse to accept the help offered by social service organizations. Still others might be perfectly healthy and choose not to work but to live on the generosity of others. What should we do in such situations? Should we still give? I remember the challenge of Bishop Untener.

No Strings Attached

Kenneth Untener was named the fourth Roman Catholic bishop of Saginaw, Michigan, in 1980 and remained so until he died of leukemia in 2004. Labeled an "ultraliberal" by his critics, he had strong views on women in the Church and society, birth control, and the development of leadership skills in clergy and laity. Much to the surprise of pastors and parishioners, immediately after his consecration as bishop, Untener sold the bishop's mansion and began the practice of living for periods of time in the rectories of his priests. This decision reflected his belief that the poor and homeless should be welcomed in parishes just as Jesus had surrounded himself with the needy of his time.

As a young friar studying for the priesthood, I had the privilege of meeting and attending a lecture by Bishop Untener at Catholic Theological Union in the early 1980s. He spoke on why we need the poor in our lives and what we can learn from them.

During a question and answer session after his lecture, a man raised his hand and said, "Bishop, I work in Chicago's Loop. Every morning as I walk from the train station to the office, I encounter numerous panhandlers. And they are the same people each and every day. Come rain or shine, they are there hustling for my pocket change. I can't help but think these people are millionaires because of the tax-free donations they receive every day. I believe the vast majority are scammers who are taking advantage of us."

"And your question is?" the bishop asked.

"Well, I don't have a question. I guess I just wanted to offer you my opinion."

"It's noted," the bishop said and continued, "I think it's important to remember that a lot of the people on the street suffer from some form of mental illness. Still others have fallen on incredibly difficult times. And then there are—as you call them—the 'scammers.' It's impossible to know who's who. But I do know that when society forces people to live on the streets to scratch out an existence, they quickly develop their own methods of survival and sometimes learn the art of the con game. So be it! But in each case, we are never exempt from offering charity. Jesus makes it clear that we are to give to whoever asks of us. Consider it a blessing to be called a fool for charity."

Bishop Untener reiterated the teaching of Jesus: "Give to everyone who begs from you, and do not refuse anyone who wants to borrow from you" (Matthew 5:42). The risk of wasting our time or being taken advantage of should not stop us from following in the footsteps of the Lord and Divine Master. We give with no strings attached. Soul training in generous and charitable sharing is a fundamental and practical consequence of the kenotic selflessness of God's instruments.

And lest we forget, all our sacrifices and acts of charity form the measuring stick of our own receptivity. "Give, and it will be given to you. A good measure, pressed down, shaken together, running over, will be put into your lap; for the measure you give will be the measure you get back" (Luke 6:38). I think of it as the karma of charity: we receive what we give.

The Peace Prayer states the promise of God and the reality in life succinctly: "It is in giving that we receive." And perhaps it offers a further challenge as Bishop Untener reminded his audience: the compliment of being considered a fool for charity.

....
CUSTOMIZE YOUR TRAINING

- Which charitable organization do you contribute to on a regular basis? Why have you chosen this organization?
- What's your reaction to Bishop Untener's statement that we are never exempt from the law of charity? When have you been considered a fool for charity? How did it make you feel?

....

SPIRITUAL COOLDOWN

Ponder

The point is this: the one who sows sparingly will also reap sparingly, and the one who sows bountifully will also reap bountifully. Each of you must give as you have made up your mind, not reluctantly or under compulsion, for God loves a cheerful giver. (2 Corinthians 9:6–7)

Imitate

When [Francis] was returning from Siena on one occasion, he met a beggar at a time when he himself was wearing a short cloak over his habit because he was not well. At the sight of the poor man's destitution, Francis said to his companion, "We'll have to give this cloak back to that poor beggar, because it belongs to him. We only got it on loan until we found someone in greater need of it." His companion, however, knew well that the saint himself needed the cloak badly and he was reluctant to see him neglect himself while providing for someone else. "But," protested the saint, "God the great Almsgiver will regard it as a theft on my part, if I do not give what I have to someone who needs it more." Whenever he received anything for his needs from a benefactor, he always used to ask permission to give the article away, if he met someone poorer than himself. He spared absolutely nothing—cloaks, habits, books, or altar-cloths—as long as he was in a position to do so, he gave them all to the poor, in order to obey the commandment of love; and when he met beggars carrying heavy loads on the road, he often took the weight on his own weak shoulders. (Bonaventure, *The Major Legend of Saint Francis*, 8:5)

Pray

Lord and Divine Master, may your grace stretch the size of my heart so I can share generously and spontaneously with any needy person you send into my life. Amen.

....

CHAPTER ELEVEN

It Is in Dying that We Are Born to Eternal Life

I did not know this was going to be my last visit with Martin before his funeral.

"How are you?"

"Frankly, Father, for the past couple of weeks, I was filled with sadness and self-pity. I was having a hard time confronting the fact that I probably won't see my fiftieth birthday. This is probably my last lap. I've had a wonderful life and was so hoping to get at least another twenty-five years. But it's not going to happen. So I was really focused on the end.

"But then my niece visited me the other day. She brought along her six-month-old daughter. Because of the cancer, I was too sick to attend her baptism or the party afterward. I asked my niece about little Alice's birth, and she said something that struck me. She said, 'Uncle Martin, it went like a charm. Alice just let go, slid down the birth canal, and popped into our family.' And then she added, 'It's just like dying, don't you think?'"

"What do you mean? I asked her."

"'Well,'" she said, "'death is just like being born—or maybe I should say, it's another birth, a new beginning. You must let go of this world. Like an infant, you slide through a birth canal. That's what the dying process is all about. Then, suddenly, you pop out into eternal life. And then you become aware of a whole new identity with the communion of saints as your family.'"

"I've been thinking about what my niece said, Father. And it's so true. We are born. We experience this life. We die. And then we are born again. Why fight the inevitable when the inevitable is what we have been preparing for all along? It's only been a few days since my niece's visit, but what she said taught me how to die."

I was intrigued. "What do you mean? How does one die?"

"The secret is to pray daily for the grace to let go. Over the past fifteen months, I've seen my freedom, independence, and privacy fade as I've become bedridden. I fought those losses tooth and nail every day and that made me so restless and unhappy. But since my niece's visit, I've begun my birthing technique, if you will, of letting go and surrendering. I'm working on them becoming a habit for me. That way, when death comes knocking at my door, it will be another moment of doing what hopefully will become second nature to me—letting go and surrendering."

Martin taught me the secret to a happy death. And, as I mentioned in his funeral homily two weeks later, he also taught me that letting go and surrendering are the secrets to living as well.

THE FIRST DEATH

Soul training requires asceticism. The Greek root for "asceticism," *ascesis*, ("to practice"), comes from the ancient world of sports and suggests there are necessary techniques to practice that help us respond to the gratuity of grace and thus attain our goal. Paul reminded the Corinthians of our goal: "Athletes exercise self-control in all things; they do it to receive a perishable wreath, but we an imperishable one" (1 Corinthians 9:25).

Our imperishable crown, received after crossing the finish line, is birth into eternal life. Paul tells us that we are mortals on the way to immortality (see 1 Corinthians 15:42–57). But crossing that finish line is no easy feat. It requires two distinct moments of letting go and surrendering, two distinct deaths.

The first death is kenotic selflessness—"denying oneself" and "losing oneself" (see Matthew 16:24–25) in imitation of Jesus who "emptied himself" (Philippians 2:7). This is the movement from a centripetal to a centrifugal stance as we surrender, sacrifice, and serve as well as let go of our fears, attachments, control issues, and sense of entitlement. The three traditional ascetical practices of Jesus—prayer, fasting, and almsgiving (see Matthew 6:1–18)—help train our souls in this kenotic selflessness.

PRAYER
Poor Clare nuns, cloistered Carmelite nuns, Trappist monks, hermits, and the multitude of people committed to prayer follow the footsteps of the Lord and Divine Master into solitary places (see Matthew 14:23; Luke 22:41). That commitment is hard work—in fact, it can be a demanding ascetical practice.

Prayer is one way we relate to God and respond to the gratuity of grace. It is calling to mind and living with the awareness of the divine presence that surrounds us like the air we breathe. As we grow in that awareness, we open ourselves to a transformative relationship. And like any other relationship, it requires commitment (we must spend time in prayer on a regular basis), communication (we must be willing to be transparent and honest with God), and compromise (sooner or later we must learn to let go of our prayer techniques and need for control in order for the Spirit to pray within us).

Prayer also challenges us to face the personality props that we idolize and that hinder us from responding to the gratuity of grace. It sometimes impels us to let go of our fears and sense of entitlement and then trains our souls to catch the centrifugal force of the Spirit. Leading us to surrender, prayer gives us the ability to die to our desires and say with the Lord and Divine Master, "Not my will but yours be done" (Luke 22:42).

FASTING

Fasting from food challenges us to die to the physical demands of our bodies and trains us in self-control and moderation. Jesus reminds us that it should not become a public display that bolsters a sense of spiritual entitlement:

> And whenever you fast, do not look dismal, like the hypocrites, for they disfigure their faces so as to show others they are fasting. Truly I tell you, they have received their reward. But when you fast, put oil on your head and wash your face, so that your fasting may be seen not by others but by your Father who is in secret; and your Father who sees in secret will reward you. (Matthew 6:16–18).

Traditionally, the money saved while fasting is given to the poor and needy. Consequently, like prayer, it too helps us catch the centrifugal force of the Spirit as we look beyond ourselves and then share what we have with the less fortunate.

Fasting and sharing is not limited to food and the money saved. Josephina reminds me that it is the decision to deny not only one's appetites but also one's wishes, desires, and daily routine. After working a long, hard day in a restaurant kitchen, she goes home. Instead of watching her favorite television program to relax, Josephina will sometimes "fast" from it and spend time helping her children with their homework. Her fasting is shaping her kenotic selflessness.

ALMSGIVING

Almsgiving trains our souls in acts of selfless surrender, self-denying sacrifice, and solicitous service. Done in secret and without ostentation (see Matthew 6:1–4), it is not limited to the sharing of our treasure. Denise offers the alms of her time and babysits for free so young couples who can't afford a babysitter can have a date night. Daniel shares his talent by offering free tax services to senior citizens. Almsgiving is about investing in the life of another.

Writing to the Corinthians about the collection for the poor of Jerusalem, Paul highlights the generosity of the Macedonian churches (Philippi and Thessalonica) who, despite their extreme poverty, "in a severe test of affliction ... overflowed in a wealth of generosity on their part" (2 Corinthians 8:2). In a surprising and stunning interpretation, he compares those churches' generous almsgiving to the birth and death of Jesus: "For you know the generous act of our Lord Jesus Christ, that though he was rich, yet for your sakes he became poor, so that by his poverty you might become rich" (v. 9). Almsgiving imitates the Lord and Divine Master's kenotic selflessness.

Each in its own way, prayer, fasting, and almsgiving help us let go of our selfishness and self-centeredness often embodied in our fears, attachments, control issues, and sense of entitlement. We die to ourselves as we catch the centrifugal force of the Spirit. This is the first death that brings us up to the finish line. But the imperishable crown is not yet ours. It takes what Francis of Assisi called in the Canticle of the Creatures "the second death"[46] to finish the race.

The Second Death

Death is always confronting us: when a friend dies, when we or a loved one are diagnosed with a terminal disease, or when we watch the nightly news reports that detail wars, local tragedies, and natural disasters. No matter the instance, many of us fear death or live in denial of it because, like Martin, we initially think of it as the termination of our existence. But is it really the end?

While studying the Chinese language in Taiwan, I took a four-day trip to Alishan National Scenic Area, a mountain resort and nature reserve famous for its mountain wilderness, waterfalls, and hiking trails. I remember looking out onto a huge field that once held hundreds of Formosan cypress trees, some as tall as 190 feet with diameters of 23 feet. Now those majestic trees were reduced to hundreds of three-inch-high stumps. After the cession of Taiwan to Japan at the conclusion of the First Sino-Japanese War in 1895, Japanese expeditions discovered the large trees and developed the logging industry to export them. A century later, in the summer of 1992, I saw something incredible: small shoots of green were emerging from those three-inch-high stumps. The trees were coming back to life.

Since the Middle Ages, nature has been considered the first book of revelation written by God. It not only gives us insights about our Creator but also gives us hints of the continuation of life after death. The change of weather in the cycle of the four seasons testifies to the yearly renewal of nature. Some plants go dormant in the winter and come back to life in the spring. Some animals, like bears, go into hibernation only to emerge in the spring. The caterpillar stops eating, hangs upside down from a twig, and molts into a shiny chrysalis or spins itself a cocoon; within its protective casing, the caterpillar's body is radically transformed, eventually emerging as a butterfly or moth with the ability to defy gravity. Jesus himself pointed to nature when he taught about the continuation of life after death: "Very truly, I tell you, unless a grain of wheat falls into the earth and dies, it remains just a single grain; but if it dies, it bears much fruit. Those who love their life lose it, and those who hate their life in this world will keep it for eternal life" (John 12:24–25). It seems to be a law of nature: death gives way to life. Always.

FROM GETHSEMANE TO THE EMPTY TOMB

God's instruments know, as my dying friend Martin's experience attests, that the footsteps of the Lord and Divine Master lead to a garden of agony where we must come to grips with the reality of death. As Martin initially did, some people see death as the end; sadly, as we sometimes witness in intensive care units, they spend the final moments of their earthly lives fighting against the inevitable and thus missing the opportunity to die in peace. It is the rare person who, due to tragic or sudden death, escapes the mental confrontation—but not the reality.

As Martin's dying days also bear out, the footsteps of the Lord and Divine Master lead beyond the garden of Gethsemane. After confronting the reality of death and overcoming its fear—"Father, if you are willing, remove this cup from me; yet, not my will but yours be done" (Luke 22:42)—Jesus looked beyond himself to the will of God. He surrendered to everything: from the kiss of betrayal to the mockery of the soldiers as he hung upon the cross. In his final hours, he was still interceding for and selflessly ministering to the needs of others: "Father, forgive them; for they do not know what they are doing" (Luke 23:34). "Woman, here is your son.... Here is your mother" (John 19:26–27). His dying moments were not the beginning of the end but a continuation of what he had been doing all his life. Still clearing an interior space and emptying himself, Jesus offered one final act of kenotic selflessness, "Father, into your hands I commend my spirit" (Luke 23:46). Even as he breathed his last, he was looking beyond himself, letting go, and surrendering to the Father's will. And in response to the gracious gift of his life, the Father raised him up. His life continued—and continues! "I was dead, and see, I am alive forever and ever" (Revelation 1:18). Death gives way to life. Always.

"If we have died with him, we will also live with him" (2 Timothy 2:11). As Martin reminded me in his final days, our soul training prepares us for the transition into eternal life. To the degree that we have practiced the first death, the second death becomes another moment of responding to the gratuity of grace by selflessly letting go and surrendering.

The Peace Prayer concludes with a simple reminder: "For it is in dying that we are born to eternal life." More than a mere summary of the prayer's second stanza with its call to kenotic selflessness, this verse points to the resurrection, the foundation of Christian hope knitted into the very sinews of every deciduous ash, aspen, beech, birch, cherry, elm, and hickory tree. Perhaps the ancient Greeks and Romans had intuited God's revelation in the book of nature: the Olympic crown, the perishable wreath referred to by Paul in the first letter to the Corinthians, was woven of *evergreen* laurel branches, perhaps foreshadowing the imperishable crown of eternity. Life never ends. Never.

Francis of Assisi, like the Lord and Divine Master, spent his life practicing the first death of asceticism in preparation for the second death: He decided to serve the Master and not the servant. He renounced his clothes and family inheritance before the bishop and citizens of Assisi. He kissed the lepers and washed their sores. He taught and lived that true and perfect joy was found in letting go of fears, attachments, control issues, and a sense of entitlement. As he lay dying, he looked beyond himself and exclaimed, "Welcome, Sister Death!"[47] Indeed, he had no fear of that moment. He had sung in his Canticle of the Creatures, "Happy those [Sister Death] finds doing your will! The second death can do no harm to them."[48] Francis was being born into eternal life. The race was now finished. The victor's imperishable crown was his. Forever.

....

CUSTOMIZE YOUR TRAINING

- How often do you pray, fast, and give alms? How is each training your soul in the first death of kenotic selflessness?
- How do you feel about your own physical death? What experiences have helped you come to grips with its reality?

Ponder

Do you not know that all of us who have been baptized into Christ Jesus were baptized into his death? Therefore we have been buried with him by baptism into death, so that, just as Christ was raised from the dead by the glory of the Father, so we too might walk in newness of life.

For if we have been united with him in a death like his, we will certainly be united with him in a resurrection like his. (Romans 6:3–5)

Imitate

Then [Francis] spent the few days that remained before his death in praise, teaching his companions whom he loved so much to praise Christ with him... . He also invited all creatures to praise God, and by means of the words he had composed earlier, he exhorted them to love God. He exhorted death itself, terrible and hateful to all, to give praise, and going joyfully to meet it, he invited it to make its lodging with him. "Welcome," he said, "my sister death." To the doctor he said: "Tell me bravely, brother doctor, that death, which is the gateway of life, is at hand." (Thomas of Celano, *The Second Life of Saint Francis*, 217)

Pray

Lord and Divine Master, grant me the grace to selflessly die to my wishes and desires so that, with you and the communion of saints, I might enjoy the gift of eternal life. Amen.

....

Amen

A beloved and treasured prayer for a century, the Peace Prayer has been ascribed to Saint Francis of Assisi though, in fact, it was probably written seven centuries after his death. In fourteen simple verses, it captures the essence of soul training.

Soul training is our response to the gratuity of grace that never expires and is never exhausted. The initial training can be tedious and difficult since we are born selfish and self-centered. The centripetal force of the ego makes us not only cling to personality props that we lean on for our self-worth but also promotes fears, attachments, control issues, and a sense of entitlement that hinder our surrender to grace.

As we allow grace to shape us into instruments of God, we are challenged to practice the kenotic selflessness of Jesus by living lives of selfless surrender, self-denying sacrifice, and solicitous service. This selflessness is also expressed in practical ways by sowing faith, hope, love, forgiveness, and joy while consoling, understanding, and enriching the lives of others. These practices activate the centrifugal force of the Spirit that invites us to a daily death of letting go and surrendering as we walk in the footsteps of the Lord and Divine Master. As this first death becomes second nature, we prepare ourselves for the second death that leads to the imperishable crown of eternal life.

A History of the Peace Prayer of Saint Francis

Some people have argued that the Peace Prayer's popularity and allure are due to its association with the famed thirteenth-century Italian saint found standing in birdbaths around the world. And yet Saint Francis had nothing to do with the composition of the prayer. The French scholar Christian Renoux has done extensive research into the origins of the prayer and aptly calls its association with Saint Francis "a riddle to be solved."[49] Let me summarize his serpentine detective work.

In 1901, a French priest, Esther Bouquerel, founded La Ligue de la Sainte-Messe (The Holy Mass League) and began publishing a small devotional magazine called *La Clochette* (*The Little Bell*). The Peace Prayer first appeared in December 1912 when Bouquerel published it in his magazine under the title "Belle Prière à faire pendant la Messe" ("A Beautiful Prayer to Say during Mass"). See Appendix 2 for the original French version with an English translation. This first version has three verses that would subsequently disappear: the first stanza includes, "Where there is discord, let me bring union" and, "Where there is error, let me bring truth"; the second stanza includes, "It is in forgetting ourselves, that we find." Though the author of the prayer is unnamed, Renoux finds it plausible that it might have been Father Bouquerel himself.

Some scholars have noted the stylistic resemblance of the first stanza of the prayer to Saint Francis's twenty-seventh Admonition:

Where there is Love and Wisdom,
  there is neither Fear nor Ignorance.
Where there is Patience and Humility,
  there is neither Anger nor Annoyance.
Where there is Poverty and Joy,
  there is neither Cupidity nor Avarice.
Where there is Peace and Contemplation,
  there is neither Care nor Restlessness.
Where there is the Fear of God to guard the dwelling,
  there no enemy can enter.
Where there is Mercy and Prudence,
  there is neither Excess nor Harshness.[50]

The argument for a stylistic resemblance is weak. The prayer's first stanza speaks about bringing a virtue to a place where a particular vice or negative emotion reigns; the Admonition praises a combination of virtues and notes their emotional or spiritual effect on a person.

Other scholars have noted that the second stanza of the original prayer has a stylistic resemblance to this saying of Brother Giles of Assisi, one of the early companions to Saint Francis:

Blessed is he who loveth and doth not therefore desire to be loved; blessed is he who feareth and doth not therefore desire to be feared; blessed is he who serveth and doth not therefore desire to be served; blessed is he who behaveth well toward others and doth not desire that others behave well toward him; and because these are great things the foolish do not rise to them.[51]

The stylistic resemblance of noting the contrary might be a literary coincidence and reflects a common technique used even by Jesus: "For the Son of Man came not to be served but to serve…" (Mark 10:45). "Indeed, God did not send the Son into the world to condemn the world, but in order that the world might be saved through him" (John 3:17); "Do not think that I have come to abolish the law or the prophets; I have come not to abolish but to fulfill" (Matthew 5:17); "Do you think that I have come to bring peace to the earth? No, I tell you, but rather division!" (Luke 12:51)

According to Renoux's research in the Vatican Archives, the French Marquis Stanislas de La Rochethulon saw this prayer in the January 1913 edition of the *Annales de Notre-Dame de la Paix à Beauchêne (Orne)* edited by a canon, Louis Boissey. Boissey, a subscriber to *La Clochette*, rightly credited the magazine with the prayer. The marquis sent this prayer, considering it a prayer "to the Sacred Heart inspired by the testament of William the Conqueror, Rouen Saint-Gervais, 9 Sept. 1087"[52] via Vatican Secretary of State, Pietro Cardinal Gasparri, to Pope Benedict XV in December 1915. [As a young Franciscan novice taking a course on the writings of Saint Francis at Saint Bonaventure University in the summer of 1976, I recorded in my class notes that our professor, the Franciscan scholar Fr. Ignatius Brady, O.F.M, said an early version of the Peace Prayer was found in the prayer book of William the Conqueror. Brady was wrong and mistakenly took the marquis's belief about a possible inspiration as fact.]

The prayer appeared in Italian translation on the front page of the January 20, 1916, edition of the Vatican newspaper, *L'Osservatore Romano*. As World War I raged in Europe, that week's edition of the newspaper published certain prayers for peace addressed to the Sacred Heart and encouraged by the pope.

Renoux notes the "psychologizing" shift from the French original, "it is in self-forgetting that one finds," to the Italian translation, "it is in forgetting oneself that one finds oneself."

The Italian version is translated back into French with the
additional psychological shift, "it is in giving of oneself that one
receives." It was published on page 6 of the January 28, 1916,
edition of the Parisian Assumptionist-sponsored daily newspaper
La Croix. Upon seeing it, the Marquis Stanislas de La Rochethulon
immediately wrote a letter to the editor, published on February 3,
1916, mistakenly informing the newspaper that this prayer was
first published in January 1913, in the *Annales de Notre-Dame
de la Paix* and wrongly crediting the canon Louis Boissey with its
composition. The marquis had forgotten that he had told Benedict
XV that, in fact, it had first appeared in *La Clochette*.

Sometime after 1918, a Capuchin Franciscan, Fr. Étienne
Benoît, was appointed visitator of the Third Order Franciscans,
known today as the Secular Franciscans, of Rheims. He had
printed a holy card for the Franciscan laity. On one side of the
card was the image of Saint Francis of Assisi and on the reverse
side the "PRIÈRE POUR LA PAIX" ("PRAYER FOR PEACE").
Underneath the prayer, Benoît mentioned how the prayer summed
up not only the character traits of the saint but also the lifestyle
of his followers. He encouraged the Tertiaries to pray this prayer
daily and to ask God for the grace to put it into practice.

Renoux believes that a French translation was made of some
other hypothetical English translation; that new French translation appeared in the September 1925 issue of *Vie franciscaine*.

In the Parisian spring of 1925, Jules Rambaud, a Protestant
pastor and reconciliation activist, introduced a slightly modified
version of the 1912 *La Clochette* original to a fellow Protestant,
Étienne Bach, a French lieutenant and founder of the Mouvement

des Chevaliers du Prince de la Paix (Movement of Knights of the Prince of Peace). The prayer was adopted as the official prayer of the Movement and published in its *Bulletin* in December 1925. Though the original title, "Une belle prière," was used, the prayer would subsequently be called the "Prière des Chevaliers de la Paix" ("Prayer of the Knights of Peace").

In August 1927, the slightly modified version received by Bach was published in the account of the third assembly of the Mouvement des Chevaliers du Prince de la Paix in Bois-Tizac, Gironde. This was the first time it was explicitly attributed to Saint Francis of Assisi. Renoux aptly notes that Protestants are the first to attribute the prayer to Saint Francis.

The first English translation was published earlier that year in January. "A prayer of St. Francis of Assissi" (*sic*) appeared in *Friends' Intelligencer*, published by the Religious Society of Friends, commonly known as the Quakers.[53] See Appendix 3 for this translation in its original format. Nine years later, it appeared in the book *Living Courageously* by Kirby Page, a Disciple of Christ minister, peace activist, and author of more than twenty-five books. For many years, it was wrongly believed that Page had introduced the prayer to the English-speaking world.

Young India, a periodical edited by Mahadev Desai, the personal secretary of Mahatma Gandhi, published a version of the prayer and credited it to "St. Francis of Assissi" (*sic*) in January 1932. He acknowledged he had received it from two Christian friends.[54] Two years later, Desai published a biography of Saint Francis.

In August 1932, a shortened version of the English prayer was published in the "Boy Scouts Bulletin" section of a newspaper called *The Daily Gleaner* of Kingston, Jamaica. Under a section head titled "Happifying Service" to inspire Rover Scouts, the anonymous writer notes:

"Francis of Assissi's [*sic*] prayer may well be that of a Rover where he says:

> Lord make me an instrument of thy peace,
>   Where there is hatred let me sow love,
>   Where there is sadness let me sow joy
>   O Divine Master,
>   *Grant that I may not so much seek*
>   *To be consoled, as to console;*
>   *To be understood, as to understand,*
>   *To be loved, as to love.*"[55]

One can only wonder if the italics of the second part of the prayer were the writer's attempt to emphasize what he thought was most important.

If ever you find yourself in Saint Francis's hometown of Assisi browsing in one of the many gift shops as I have on many occasions, you'll typically find the prayer associated with an image of the saint and simply called Preghiera semplice (A Simple Prayer). It seems the twenty-first-century citizens of Assisi are hesitant to give their famous thirteenth-century son credit for a prayer more than likely written at the beginning of the twentieth century.

The Earliest Version of the Peace Prayer

French original:

Seigneur, faites de moi un
   instrument de votre paix.
Là où il y a de la haine, que je
   mette l'amour.
Là où il y a l'offense, que je mette
   le pardon.
Là où il y a la discorde, que je
   mette l'union.
Là où il y a l'erreur, que je mette
   la vérité.
Là où il y a le doute, que je mette
   la foi.
Là où il y a le désespoir, que je
   mette l'espérance.
Là où il y a les ténèbres, que je
   mette votre lumière.
Là où il y a la tristesse, que je
   mette la joie.
Ô Maître, que je ne cherche pas
   tant
à être consolé qu'à consoler,
à être compris qu'à comprendre,
à être aimé qu'à aimer,
car c'est en donnant qu'on reçoit,
c'est en s'oubliant qu'on trouve,

c'est en pardonnant qu'on est
   pardonné,
c'est en mourant qu'on ressuscite à
   l'éternelle vie.

English translation:

Lord, make me an instrument of
   your peace.
Where there is hatred, let me bring
   love.
Where there is offense, let me
   bring pardon.
Where there is discord, let me
   bring union.
Where there is error, let me bring
   truth.
Where there is doubt, let me bring
   faith.
Where there is despair, let me
   bring hope.
Where there is darkness, let me
   bring your light.
Where there is sadness, let me
   bring joy.
O Master, let me not seek
   as much
to be consoled as to console,
to be understood as to understand,
to be loved as to love,
for it is in giving that one receives,
it is in self-forgetting that one
   finds,
it is in pardoning that one is
   pardoned,
it is in dying that one is raised to
   eternal life.

....

The First Known English Translation of the Peace Prayer

Lord, make me an instrument of your peace; where there is hatred, let me sow love; where there is injury, pardon; where there is discord, union; where there is doubt, faith; where there is despair, hope; where there is darkness, light; and where there is sadness, joy.

O Divine Master, grant that I may not so much seek to be consoled, as to console; to be understood, as to understand; to be loved, as to love; for it is in giving that we receive, it is in pardoning that we are pardoned, and it is in dying that we are born to eternal life. Amen.

Pope Francis's Revision of the Peace Prayer for Journalists

Lord, make us instruments of your peace.

Help us to recognize the evil latent in a communication that does not build communion.

Help us to remove the venom from our judgments.

Help us to speak about others as our brothers and sisters.

You are faithful and trustworthy; may our words be seeds of goodness for the world:

where there is shouting, let us practice listening;

where there is confusion, let us inspire harmony;

where there is ambiguity, let us bring clarity;

where there is exclusion, let us offer solidarity;

where there is sensationalism, let us use sobriety;

where there is superficiality, let us raise real questions;

where there is prejudice, let us awaken trust;

where there is hostility, let us bring respect;

where there is falsehood, let us bring truth.

Amen.

NOTES

1.   Jena Lee Nardella, "Praying for the Nation," September 4, 2012, at http://www.jenaleenardella.com/blog/2012/09/praying-for-the-nation
2.   Margaret Thatcher Foundation, "Remarks on becoming Prime Minister (St. Francis's prayer)," May 4, 1979, at https://www.margaretthatcher.org/document/104078
3.   Rev. Nicholas S. Gengaro, "Funeral Homily, The Honorable Peter W. Rodino, Jr.," St. Lucy Church, Newark, NJ, May 16, 2005, 11 a.m., as recorded in the Congressional Record, https://www.govinfo.gov/content/pkg/CRECB-2005-pt12/html/CRECB-2005-pt12-Pg16372.htm
4.   C-Span, "Pope John Paul II Arrival," October 4, 1995, at https://www.c-span.org/video/?67468-1/pope-john-paul-ii-arrival
5.   SFGate, "Text of Nancy Pelosi's speech," January 4, 2007, at https://www.sfgate.com/bayarea/article/Text-of-Nancy-Pelosi-s-speech-2625996.php
6.   Vox, "Nancy Pelosi's first speech as House speaker celebrated women's accomplishments," January 3, 2019, at https://www.vox.com/policy-and-politics/2019/1/3/18167052/nancy-pelosi-first-speech-house-speaker-democrats-women
7.   CNN Politics, "House Speaker John Boehner: 'I decided today is the day,'" September 25, 2015, at https://www.cnn.com/2015/09/25/politics/john-boehner-resigning-as-speaker/index.html
8.   Pope Francis, "Message of His Holiness Pope Francis for World Communications Day," January 24, 2018, at http://w2.vatican.va/content/francesco/en/messages/communications/documents/papa-francesco_20180124_messaggio-comunicazioni-sociali.html
9.   Francis of Assisi, "Letter to a General Chapter" in *St. Francis of Assisi: Writings and Early Biographies. English Omnibus of the Sources for the Life of St. Francis*, ed. Marion A. Habig (Chicago: Franciscan Herald Press, 1972), 108.
10.   Mother Teresa, *Mother Teresa: Come Be My Life. The Private Writings of the Saint of Calcutta*, edited and with commentary by Brian Kolodiejchuk, M.C. (New York: Doubleday, 2007), 32.
11.   William Murdock, *Find Your Own Calcutta: Living a Life of Service and Meaning in a Selfish World* (Nashville: WestBow Press, 2017), 64.
12.   Henri Nouwen, *Turn My Mourning into Dancing: Finding Hope in Hard Times*, ed. Timothy Jones (Nashville: Thomas Nelson, , 2004), 25–26.

13.   Mother Teresa of Calcutta to Malcolm Muggeridge, quoted in Malcolm Muggeridge, *Something Beautiful for God* (New York: Harper & Row, 1971), 85–86.

14.   Musei Uniti Gubbio, Chiesa di San Francesco della Pace, "History: The church and the sarcophagus of the wolf," at https://www. sanfrancescodellapace.it/en/history/ accessed April 7, 2020.

15.   Some of these insights are taken from Jean-François Godet-Calogeras, "More Than a Legend: The Wolf of Gubbio," *The Cord: A Franciscan Spiritual Review*, November/December 2002, 260–61.

16.   Patricia Treece, *A Man for Others* (San Francisco: Harper & Row, 1982), 1.

17.   Edward O'N. Hoyt, "Saint Spotlight: Maximilian Kolbe," August 11, 2018, at https://www.crs.org/resource-center/saint-spotlight-maximilian-kolbe?gclid=EAIaIQobChMIgNOUm-WF5gIVAtbACh2kyQ0 DEAAYASAAEgIPdPD_BwE

18.   Treece, *A Man for Others*, 171.

19.   Pope Paul VI, Homily for the Beatification of Maximilian Mary Kolbe, October 17, 1971, at http://www.vatican.va/content/paul-vi/it/ homilies/1971/documents/hf_p-vi_hom_19711017.html

20.   Pope John Paul II, Homily for the Canonization of Bl. Maximilian Mary Kolbe, October 10, 1982, at http://www.vatican.va/content/ john-paul-ii/it/homilies/1982/documents/hf_jp-ii_hom_19821010_ canonizzazione-kolbe.html

21.   Pax Christi International, "About Us," at https://paxchristi.net/ about-us/ accessed April 7, 2020.

22.   Francis of Assisi, "The Rule of 1221," chap. 16, in *St. Francis of Assisi: Omnibus*, 43.

23.   Mayo Clinic Staff, "Forgiveness: Letting go of grudges and bitterness," November 4, 2017, at https://www.mayoclinic.org/healthy-lifestyle/adult-health/in-depth/forgiveness/art-20047692

24.   Mayo Clinic Staff, "Forgiveness: Letting go of grudges and bitterness," November 4, 2017.

25.   Francis of Assisi, "Letter to a Minister," in *St. Francis of Assisi: Omnibus*, 110.

26.   Francis of Assisi, "The Prayer before the Crucifix," in Francis of Assisi, Early Documents: vol. 1, *The Saint*, ed. Regis J. Armstrong, J. Wayne Hellmann, William J. Short (New York: New City Press, 1999), 40.

27.   Serena Marshall, Lana Zak, and Jennifer Metz, "Doctor compares conditions for unaccompanied children at immigrant holding centers to

'torture facilities'," June 23, 2019, at https://abcnews.go.com/Politics/doctor-compares-conditions-immigrant-holding-centers-torture-facilities/story?id=63879031.

28. Julian of Norwich, *Revelation of Love*, ed. John Skinner (New York: Doubleday, 1997), 54–55, 124.

29. *The Legend of Perugia* 43 in *St. Francis of Assisi: Omnibus*, 1021.

30. Francis of Assisi, "The Canticle of Brother Sun" in *St. Francis of Assisi: Omnibus*, 130.

31. Francis of Assisi, "The Canticle of Brother Sun" 130.

32. Francis of Assisi, "The Canticle of Brother Sun" 131.

33. Francis of Assisi, "The Canticle of Brother Sun" 131.

34. Francis of Assisi, "The Canticle of Brother Sun" 131.

35. Thomas of Celano, *The Second Life of St. Francis* 125 in *St. Francis of Assisi: Omnibus*, 466.

36. Thomas of Celano, *The Second Life of St. Francis* 125, 465.

37. Thomas of Celano, *The Second Life of St. Francis* 125, 465.

38. Thomas of Celano, *The Second Life of St. Francis* 125, 466.

39. *Mirror of Perfection* 58 in *St. Francis of Assisi: Omnibus*, 1184.

40. Thomas of Celano, *The First Life of Saint Francis* 16 in *St. Francis of Assisi: Omnibus*, 242.

41. Francis of Assisi, "The Rule of 1221," chapter 7, in *St. Francis of Assisi: Omnibus*, 38.

42. Enid R. Spitz, "The Three Kinds of Empathy: Emotional, Cognitive, Compassionate," at https://blog.heartmanity.com/the-three-kinds-of-empathy-emotional-cognitive-compassionate accessed April 7, 2020.

43. The incident, paraphrased by the author, is found in *The Legend of Perugia 1* in *St. Francis of Assisi: Omnibus*, 977.

44. Francis of Assisi, "The Testament," in *St. Francis of Assisi: Omnibus*, 67.

45. Jeanne Schatzlein, OSF, RN, MA and Daniel P. Sulmassy, OFM, MD, "The Diagnosis of St. Francis: Evidence for Leprosy." *Franciscan Studies*, 47 (1987):181-217.

46. Francis of Assisi, "The Canticle of Brother Sun," in *St. Francis of Assisi: Omnibus*, 131.

47. *Legend of Perugia* 65 in *St. Francis of Assisi: Omnibus*, 1042.

48. Francis of Assisi, "The Canticle of Brother Sun," in *St. Francis of Assisi: Omnibus*, 131.

49. Dr. Christian Renoux, *La Prière de la Paix Attribuée à Saint Francois: Une Énigme à Résourdre* (Paris: Editions Franciscaines, 2001).

50. Francis of Assisi, "The Admonitions," in *St. Francis of Assisi: Omnibus,* 86.

51. Giles of Assisi, *The Golden Sayings of Blessed Brother Giles,* translated by Paschal Robinson (Philadelphia, Dolphin Press, 1907), 5.

52. «Le preghiere del 'Souvenir Normand' per la pace». *L'Osservatore Romano* (in Italian). 20 January 1916. p. 1.

53. *Friends' Intelligencer*, 1927 First Month 22, Page 66, Column 1, Volume 84, Number 4, Religious Society of Friends, Philadelphia.

54. *Young India: A Weekly Journal*, edited by Mahadev Desai, Page 4, Column 1, Volume 14, Number 1, Navajivan Publishing House, Ahmedabad, India.

55. *The Daily Gleaner*, Boy Scouts Bulletin, Page 21, Column 2, Kingston, Jamaica.

Franciscan Media is a nonprofit ministry of the Franciscan Friars of St. John the Baptist Province. Through the publication of spiritual books, *St. Anthony Messenger* magazine, and online media properties such as *Saint of the Day, Minute Meditations,* and *Faith & Family,* Franciscan Media seeks to share God's love in the spirit of St. Francis of Assisi. For more information, to support us, and to purchase our products, visit franciscanmedia.org.

Live in love. Grow in faith.

ABOUT THE AUTHOR

Ordained a Franciscan priest in 1983, Albert Haase, OFM, is a popular preacher, teacher, and spiritual director. A former missionary to mainland China for over eleven years, he is the award-winning author of twelve books on popular spirituality and the presenter on five bestselling DVDs. He has trained spiritual directors for ten years. He is currently chaplain at Cedarbrake Catholic Retreat Center in the diocese of Austin, Texas. Visit his website at www.AlbertOFM.org